Ghostly Tales of Ohio

Dedication:
To everyone who helps to preserve history and to keep the legends alive.

Content Warning: This book contains retellings of historical events. Some tales include references to suicide, murder, and abuse and may not be appropriate for all audiences.

Cover design by Jonathan Norberg
Text design by Karla Linder
Edited by Ryan Jacobson and Emily Beaumont
Proofread by Jenna Barron

All images copyrighted.
Shelley Anderson: 134; **Brianna Royle Koqka:** 135
Images used under license from Shutterstock.com:
Covers and silhouettes: **Polina Katrich:** branches; **Morspective:** crow; **Elena Pimonova:** tree
Interior: **Antilo:** 1; **Fer Gregory:** 51; **Raggedstone:** 103; **Cait Thompson:** 33; **Arend Trent:** 75

10 9 8 7 6 5 4 3 2 1
Ghostly Tales of Ohio
Copyright © 2025 by Jessica Freeburg and Natalie Fowler
Published by Adventure Publications
An imprint of AdventureKEEN
310 Garfield Street South
Cambridge, Minnesota 55008
(800) 678-7006
www.adventurepublications.net
All rights reserved
Printed in the USA
LCCN 2025022760 (print); 2025022761 (ebook)
ISBN 978-1-64755-542-9 (pbk.); 978-1-64755-543-6 (ebook)

Ghostly Tales of Ohio

Jessica Freeburg & Natalie Fowler

Adventure PUBLICATIONS

Table of Contents

Acknowledgments	vi
Preface	vii

HAUNTED INSTITUTIONS

Ohio State Reformatory (Mansfield)	3
Gore Orphanage (Vermilion)	10
The Collingwood Arts Center (Toledo)	16
Sedamsville Rectory (Cincinnati)	20
Lake Erie College (Painsville)	24
Licking County Historic Jail (Newark)	28

HAUNTED MEDICAL FACILITIES

The Molly Stark Sanatorium (Louisville)	35
The Willoughby Medical Center (Willoughby)	40
The Ridges (Athens)	45

HAUNTED HOTELS & HISTORIC BUSINESSES

Buxton Inn (Granville)	53
The Lafayette Hotel (Marietta)	58
Park Hotel (Put-in-Bay)	62
Punderson Manor (Newbury Township)	65
The Golden Lamb (Lebanon)	68
The Akron Civic Theater (Akron)	71

HAUNTED HOUSES & MANSIONS
    Franklin Castle (Cleveland) — 77
    Ceely Rose House, Malabar Farm State Park (Lucas) — 83
    Stetson House (Waynesville) — 89
    The Kelton House Museum (Columbus) — 93
    Prospect Place (Trinway) — 97

HAUNTED OUTDOOR SPACES
    Moonville Tunnel (McArthur) — 105
    Collinwood School Fire (Collinwood) — 109
    Frankenstein's Castle (Kettering) — 115
    Spring House Gazebo in Eden Park (Cincinnati) — 120

Bibliography — 125
About Jessica Freeburg — 134
About Natalie Fowler — 135

Acknowledgments

The authors would like to thank several people who made this book possible.

We want to start by thanking the amazing team at AdventureKEEN. We deeply appreciate your partnership in creating these books.

We'd also like to thank everyone who has reported their experiences. It might have been easier to rationalize your paranormal encounter or pretend it never happened. Your stories give voice to those who can no longer speak for themselves and add rich layers to the legends of these historic locations.

We give a special shout-out to Darrin Smith for taking the time to share his vast knowledge about the Licking County Historic Jail and for the work he does to preserve the location's history. Your dedication ensures that the stories—both historical and haunted—are never forgotten. Thanks to people like you, the spirits of the past still have a voice.

And finally, to our literary agent Dawn Frederick—thank you for always believing in us and having our backs.

Preface

Ohio was first inhabited by European settlers in the mid-1700s, but its history dates back at least 14,000 years, when prehistoric hunters made their homes in what is now the Ohio River Valley. A number of Indigenous peoples planted roots in the region, rich with natural resources that allowed them to thrive. By the time Europeans arrived, area tribes included the Chippewa, Delaware, Iroquois, Miami, Mingo, Ottawa, Shawnee, and Wyandot. The influx of settlers led to the Northwest Indian War between 1785 and 1795, during which Native Americans fought to retain their homeland. With thousands of years of history, countless lives lost, and heated battles on the land, it's no wonder Ohio is a state brimming with haunted legends.

From the worn walls and stained corridors of the historic Ohio Reformatory, where an estimated 154,000 inmates served sentences for some of the most heinous crimes, to the repurposed hallways of the former Athens Asylum, where patients with psychiatric disabilities once endured lobotomies and shock therapy, the echoes of the past whisper into the present. We may never understand why some souls seem to linger, their spirits caught in a tide that pulls them to a specific place again and again. Whatever the reason, it seems that some souls don't find eternal rest. They are bound to the locations they knew in life, drawn by tethers of joy and sorrow.

Every ghost story is also the story of a life once lived. It is the echo of a heart that once beat, the whisper of a secret waiting to be heard, and a reminder that that—even in death—the human spirit perseveres.

—Jessica Freeburg and Natalie Fowler

Haunted Institutions

Ohio State Reformatory
Mansfield

January 30, 1960

Twenty-two-year-old James Lockhart exhaled slowly, his lips trembling. The smell of lighter fluid burned his nostrils as he steadied himself for what came next.

James had been a teen when he first came to the Ohio State Reformatory on October 5, 1955, to serve a 1- to 15-year sentence for what the judge called assault with intent to kill. James spent part of that time at Lima State Hospital, getting treatment for his psychiatric disorders. Life had never been easy for him, but life locked within the concrete walls of a 7x9-foot cell was more than he could take.

He closed his eyes and listened to the buzz of inmates making their way to supper.

"Are you coming, Lockhart?" a guard called from outside Cell 13.

"No, sir," James replied, his senses heightened by a rush of adrenaline as he rubbed his thumb against the cool metal of the lighter clutched in his hand. It was nice to hear a guard call him by name rather than by number. There was something about being called "54673" that left him feeling like a piece of inventory rather than a human. But he supposed that was the point.

"What's that smell?" James's neighbor asked, standing at the front of his cell, breathing in the distinctly pungent odor of the accelerant James had splashed on his bedding a moment earlier.

James knew that if his neighbor could smell the lighter fluid, it wouldn't be long before one of the guards caught wind and tried to stop him. It was now or never. He flipped open the hood of the lighter, slid his thumb against the spark wheel, and let the flame lick the corner of his bedsheet. A single flame danced lightly as the cotton caught fire and began to burn.

James turned and faced the front of his cell before dumping the remainder of the fluid on his clothing. The liquid dripped from his sleeves onto the concrete floor with a hollow splat.

"Whatcha doing, man?" the neighbor asked, his voice thick with alarm. "Don't you smell that?" the man shouted toward a guard. "He's gonna burn the whole place down!" His voice cracked on the last word.

James listened to the guard's footsteps rushing toward his cell. When the flame on his bedding reached the area soaked with lighter fluid, the fire burst to life. Searing heat filled the small room.

The neighbor screamed as a flash of fire shot from James's cell into his. The singed skin on his hands bubbled into blisters as he stumbled to his sink and began splashing water on himself.

Two guards, Paul Sheeks and John Fraunfelter, stood on the other side of James's cell, their eyes wide with shock. James faced the stunned guards as he backed slowly toward the corner of the tiny room.

"Don't do it, Lockhart!"

His name again. For another moment, he was more than a number. But that didn't matter. He knew what they did with the bodies of inmates nobody wanted—and he was certain no one would want his. They stuck those bodies in the ground out back with nothing but their number marking the final resting place. He doubted anyone would remember that 54673 was once a man called James Lockhart, and he was sure that no one would care.

James's heart raced as he held the lighter under his dripping sleeve.

As the guards stepped toward his cell door to open it, flames from the bedding leapt wildly at them, melting the polyester of their cuffed uniforms onto their wrists. Their faces were seared by the ungodly heat. They screamed in pain as they moved away from the red-hot iron bars.

James flicked his thumb across the wheel one last time, turning his cell into an incinerator.

* * *

February 7, 1960

William sat at the desk near the closed door of the east cell block, reading the local paper. He stared at the headline: "Inmate Burns Self to Death at OSR." The article was short—just six paragraphs—a snapshot of the horror that had unfolded just a few hundred feet from where William sat now.

"I can't even drink my coffee," his coworker Glen grumbled, dropping his thermos onto the desk before picking up a clipboard and signing in. "Smells so bad in this place, I can taste it."

The smell of burned flesh hung in the air like a nightmare from which they couldn't wake.

"I'm not going to disagree with you," William replied, closing the paper and setting it beside Glen's thermos. "Let's get morning cell check done."

The guards made their way to their assigned floors. William stood at the end of the north side of the level-four tier, surveying the cells ahead of him. The sound of a toilet flushed. Then another flushed nearby. Water plinked into metal sinks as inmates washed the sleep from their eyes or brushed their teeth. Most of the men kept themselves up pretty well. William figured that perhaps it was one of the few things that made them feel normal.

He took a few steps onto the walkway, joining the echoed footsteps of the other guards, making the same journey on different tiers. He focused his attention on the cells he needed to check.

"Morning, Jack." He nodded into the first cell.

The inmate nodded back. "That it is," Jack replied.

William found his job less stressful if he treated the inmates with respect. After the horror of last week, he was more acutely aware of their internal battles. Most of them had been young, first-time offenders when they entered the reformatory. Many, like James Lockhart, had entered the facility as 18-year-old kids and had grown into men while paying their penance.

Ghostly Tales of Ohio

William swallowed a lump that rose in his throat as he thought of James. His eyes glanced at the floor. A dark stain, like grease, was smeared under his foot. The stain started a few cells from where he presently stood, at Cell 13, and continued down the steps he'd just walked up. No matter what they tried, the stain wouldn't go away. Maybe it would fade over time, but for now, it was a grim reminder of the most horrific scene any of these men had ever witnessed.

James had been beyond hope of saving almost immediately—his body nearly indistinguishable from the flames that engulfed him. The best anyone could do was clean up the chunks of blackened flesh that slipped off his bones as the guards dragged the charred remains away from his fiery death chamber.

"I can't sleep in here," the next inmate said. He was still in bed as he looked through the bars at William.

"I know, Terry. The smell's pretty bad. It'll get better."

"It's not that," Terry replied. "Look at me."

William cocked his head and peered at the thin mattress. The sheets were tucked so tightly underneath it that Terry looked mummified—every contour of his body was visible beneath the smooth blankets. Even his arms seemed trapped under the covers.

"Well, you got yourself tucked in there real nice, I'll give you that."

"That's the problem. I didn't do this. My sheets were hanging off the side when I went to sleep. I felt hands tugging at my blankets in the middle of the night. I was so scared. I just closed my eyes and prayed whatever was doing it would go away. I woke up tucked in here like a baby. I can barely move." Terry's feet began to wiggle under the blankets, and he began to shimmy his body before kicking one leg free from the strangely constrictive sheets.

William had heard a few inmates complain over the years about someone tugging at their sheets at night. This was the first time he'd ever seen evidence of it.

"I stayed in here like this so you could see me," he said, swinging his legs off the bed, his breath fast from the effort required to get himself unbound. "I'm telling you, this place is haunted. Even before James made it stink to high heaven, there were noises out in the range keeping me up all night, footsteps and clanging when everyone's asleep, hands grabbing at me in the middle of the night."

William listened quietly.

"I'm in this cell alone. There's no one in here to grab me." Terry's eyes widened as he stood up. "How could I get myself tucked in like that? I couldn't even move my arms."

"I'm sorry, Terry. It's not that I don't believe you," William replied.

He'd had his own experiences in the prison, especially down in the hole. It wasn't just the feeling of isolation and despair that hung in the dark, dank cells where men would live in pitch blackness for days without food or water. On more than one occasion, William had been hit or pushed by unseen hands.

William often marveled at the dichotomy of this place. From the outside, the prison was beautiful. Twin front porches, centered by a turret, gave the prison the appearance of a mansion. But inside those grand walls, prisoners and guards saw the worst of humanity: riots, assaults, and even murder always remained possibilities. Hopelessness led more men than James Lockhart to take their own lives. The air was thick with anger and regret every day.

Terry turned his back to William, bringing the conversation to an end. William continued along the concrete walkway that was stained by desperation and death.

The place was haunted, but what could William do about it, other than try to keep the prisoners calm and try to bring a little humanity to their lives?

* * *

The Ohio State Reformatory opened in 1896 and would house prisoners for nearly 100 years. Although it was created with the intention of educating and reforming first-time offenders who were too old for the juvenile system, by the time the facility closed in 1990, it was a maximum-security prison, housing some of the most violent criminals in the state.

When it functioned as a true reformatory, it had a high success rate, with a low number of inmates who reoffended after serving time there. While many inmates found reformation within its walls, many others found misery and pain. Some sought release through suicide. Others released their anger as rage against guards and fellow inmates.

The bodies of more than 200 inmates who passed away were left unclaimed. Those bodies were interred in simple pine boxes made by other prisoners and buried in the prison cemetery—marked by only their prisoner number. Among them is number 54673.

Gore Orphanage
Vermilion

Fall 2023

Trees formed a wall along the left side of the road, blurring past the driver's side window. Their leaves had long since fallen to the forest floor, blanketing the patches of vegetation beneath. To the right, an open field sat empty. The yellowing grass gave the land a barren appearance.

Alex kept his eyes on the road, swerving now and then to avoid potholes. The sun dropped steadily toward the horizon, casting a golden glow across the sky.

"It is very pretty out here," Cara said from the passenger seat.

"Pretty creepy," Elizabeth replied, leaning over Thomas's shoulder to peer into the forest. She didn't expect to see a ghost child staring back at her. She knew the others wanted to see signs of the paranormal, but she secretly hoped they wouldn't. She wasn't as into ghosts as her friends were—but she was fascinated by the history.

In 1865, Nicholas Wilber purchased an ornate mansion on Gore Road that had been built by Joseph Swift. The mansion went up for sale after Joseph tragically lost two of his children and made a bad railroad investment. A known spiritualist, Nicholas was rumored to have regularly made contact with the Swift children, who had died in the home, during séances.

In 1902, religious zealot Reverend Johann Sprunger and his wife, Katharina, built the Light of Hope Orphanage on the property. They chose not to use the abandoned mansion, which had fallen into disrepair.

As many as 120 children at a time were housed at the self-sufficient farm, many of whom escaped over the years. These runaways reported deplorable conditions, including rat-infested rooms, lice, beatings, and neglect.

The Sprungers were investigated for abuse in 1909. Even though they admitted to the allegations, they were allowed to continue running the orphanage. Two years later, Reverend Sprunger died, and in 1916, the orphanage was permanently closed due to financial troubles.

Alex slowed the car as he drove over the Vermilion River bridge. The four friends noticed the graffiti-covered beams as they rolled past.

Shadows thickened in the woodland beside them, and it wasn't long before they found a crumbling sandstone pillar that was also covered in graffiti. The pillar was all that remained of an elaborate entrance to the old property. Alex parked on the side of the road.

"We have enough time to grab some footage before it gets too dark," Cara said.

The teens had gotten permission to do a project for their history class. Cara had aspirations of going into film production after high school, so she'd convinced the group to create a short documentary about the local legend.

Elizabeth took a deep breath and joined the others, clutching her notebook. She had some research to share on film; it gave her something to focus on other than ghosts.

"How many buildings are we looking for?" asked Alex, leading the others through the brush, down what used to be a road.

Thomas walked behind them, filming the trio as they walked.

"There were five buildings," said Elizabeth. "The whole Swift Hollow area is about 543 acres, and the Swift mansion was a large Greek Revival-style house. The Light of Hope Orphanage was composed of four farm buildings. The boys lived at what was called the Hughes farm, and the girls lived at the Howard farm."

"They didn't use the mansion?" asked Cara. "That's strange." She stepped over a tree branch that blocked the faint remnants of the path they followed.

"The staff might have used the mansion but not the kids or the Sprungers," Elizabeth replied. "It was already rumored to be haunted, even back then. They probably didn't want anything to do with it."

The sun dipped farther below the horizon. Elizabeth swallowed a lump in her throat as she realized they'd be walking back to the car in darkness. She returned her focus to the notebook, embracing the momentary distraction of her research.

"Get this," said Elizabeth. "When the Sprungers arrived from Indiana, they brought their dead daughter with them."

"What?" asked Alex.

"Yeah, their daughter, Hillegonda, died at age 7 in Indiana. When they moved here, they brought her body with them and reburied it."

"That's creepy," said Cara. "Do you think we can find her grave?"

"No," said Elizabeth, "because it gets even weirder. The orphanage closed in July of 1916. Most of the orphaned children were sent to live in the community or were returned to relatives. But Mrs. Sprunger took a few of them—and her dead daughter—back to Indiana."

As they continued walking, Elizabeth glanced over her shoulder, toward the trees that lined the path. A small ball of light bounced behind a tree trunk. She stopped, and so did Thomas.

"Did you see that?" Thomas whispered, stepping closer to Elizabeth. He turned his camera toward the light, which was no longer there.

"Probably just a firefly," Elizabeth reasoned.

The pair watched the tree line for a moment. When the light didn't reappear, they hustled to catch up with the others.

They came upon what remained of the Swift Mansion: a water-logged hole where the house once stood, surrounded by foundation blocks.

Thomas moved around the group, filming everyone and shooting the ruins from different angles.

Elizabeth read from her notes: "The Sprungers moved here because the orphanage they ran in Berne,

Ghostly Tales of Ohio 13

Indiana, also called the Light of Hope Orphanage, was suspiciously destroyed in a horrific fire. Three girls died in that fire. Fortunately, the fire that destroyed the Swift mansion occurred while it was empty."

Another ball of light slipped through the shadows of the tree line.

Cara gasped. "I just saw an orb."

"I saw it too," Elizabeth added. "And I saw one earlier."

Everyone stood still, watching, listening. Thomas panned the camera slowly, hoping to catch something on film.

A ball of light flashed behind him.

"There it is again!" Elizabeth cried.

Thomas spun with the camera but once again missed capturing the anomaly.

The hair on the back of Elizabeth's neck stood as she held her breath, watching for more strange orbs, her senses on overdrive. She only heard the dull buzz of highway traffic in the distance . . . until a faint scream broke the eerie silence.

The four exchanged wide-eyed glances.

Another scream, a little closer, caused all of them to break into a run back down the path toward the car. Twilight pulled the afternoon into evening, as the teens burst through the tree line and dashed to the vehicle.

As Elizabeth rushed around the back of the car, she saw several small handprints, like those of children, along the bumper.

She jumped into the backseat, too frightened to speak. The doors slammed shut, and Alex sped toward the bridge.

When they were back in town, parked in front of Cara's house, Elizabeth mentioned the handprints. They looked for any sign of them, but the bumper was covered in dust from the gravel road. If there had been any, they were no longer visible.

Could the spirits of abused children be wandering the place they were once forced to call home? The conditions they suffered through were deplorable. It was reported that they were forced to eat food most people wouldn't dream of, such as corn that was cooked in the same pot used to boil their dirty underwear. With rats crawling into the children's beds and biting them, even sleep couldn't offer a reprieve from their misery.

It's no wonder the land remains haunted more than 100 years after the institution shut down. Given the interest in this dark period of Ohio's history, ghostly sightings could continue for generations to come.

Collingwood Arts Center
Toledo

In 1872, local merchant Christian Gerber spared no expense in building a grand and opulent home on what would become Collingwood Boulevard. With elegant parlors, high ceilings, solid walnut doors, and elaborate fireplace mantels, the cost to build his home was double the projected estimates. Christian probably should have spared some expense because, by 1875, he declared bankruptcy.

The Gerber House was sold a few times until it found a new purpose. In 1905, the Ursuline Order of the Sacred Heart purchased the property. In 1922, the Ursuline Order opened Mary Manse College—the first women's Catholic college—on the premises.

Today, the second and third floors of the Gerber House are rented to artists as part of the Collingwood Arts Center. The parlors of the house are used for art exhibits and conference meetings. There are also regular theater events and historic (and haunted) tours on the property.

* * *

Fall 2022

Ashley stepped back from her painting with a critical eye. Something was off, but she couldn't figure out what it was. With a sigh, she peeked at the clock. It was 5:20 p.m.

She was supposed to have been downstairs 20 minutes ago, working on sets for the theater group. After tucking away her brushes and sealing up her paints, she wiped her spattered hands with a paint-stained cloth.

She shut the door to her studio and locked it. The sense of pride she felt about her space on the second floor seemed to grow stronger every day. It had been a dream come true to get accepted into the Collingwood Arts Center.

She hurried downstairs, admiring the painstaking renovations that had turned the nuns' vision of a women's school into its present purpose as a home for artists.

Ashley found her way into the theater. Tom, the set designer, was backstage cutting lumber. Ashley mixed the paints and was soon perched on her scaffolding, creating blue swirls for a Monet-inspired set.

Tom came out from backstage and called, "I've got to run to the hardware store. Do you need anything?"

"No, thanks," she said. "Are the others coming?"

Tom shrugged. "I think they're on artist time."

Ashley laughed. "I get that."

"I'll be back in an hour, and I'll bring tacos."

Ashley gave him a thumbs-up.

After Tom left, she became aware of the unsettling quietness. She felt overwhelmed by a sense of being alone. More than that, she felt exposed. Her mind raced with stories about how the building was "the most haunted in Toledo."

She knew that the basement was creepy. She knew that the spirit of a solemn bride roamed the hallways of the Gerber House. She knew that ghostly children ran up and down the hallways outside her studio.

None of those stories had ever concerned her—until now. As an artist, she spent a lot of time alone. She even joked that she had too much going on in her head, so there wasn't room to think about ghosts. Yet all of a sudden, ghosts were all she could think about. It was like the atmosphere had changed. She felt as if someone was watching her.

Slowly, she turned around on her scaffolding. Her eyes surveyed the seats of the theater. For a moment, she admired the vantage point from her perch. But then she saw her: A nun sat in the third row of the balcony.

Locking eyes with the ghostly being, Ashley felt judgment and hatred emanating from the woman in the habit. Ashley fought the urge to scramble down the ladder and run out of the building. She had faced plenty of critics. Many times, even people she cared about said that her dream wasn't worth chasing. Not one of those voices was louder than the critic in her head, which she battled every day. She wasn't going to let anyone—especially the ghost of a nun—judge her now.

Ashley stared back, and her fear shifted. At first it shifted into anger, but it quickly became compassion.

Finding her voice, she said, "I'm sorry for whatever happened in your life—or even in your death—that made you angry, but I have a job to do. You're welcome to watch, but if you don't like what I am doing, you are also free to leave."

Ashley dabbed her brush into the darkest of the blues and returned to her work. She wasn't sure if she wanted to know whether the nun was still there, so she resisted the urge to look over her shoulder. But the energy in the theater seemed to lighten, and soon Ashley was lost again in her work, happy to be living her dream.

Sedamsville Rectory
Cincinnati

In 1878, the Our Lady of Perpetual Help church was founded to serve Cincinnati's Sedamsville neighborhood and its growing German-Catholic population. In 1891, the parish added a rectory for priests. Over the course of the rectory's history, strange deaths were reported, including that of a priest who was struck by a train on his way to visit a sick parishioner. There were also allegations of abuse within its walls. Two bodies were found on the street out front, at different times: a man and later a child, who was wearing a noose.

In 1989, the church (and rectory) closed its doors. Six years later, the property was purchased by a developer with plans to turn it into a rental property. A lot of work was needed to bring the place back to its former beauty.

* * *

Summer 2005

Chris climbed the front steps of the vacant brick building and fished the key out of his pocket. He jiggled it in the lock, and the door eventually swung open.

The bright summer daylight filled the hallway, chasing away the shadows. Chris was startled by the stillness inside. He'd been in a lot of abandoned places, but this was his first time in the rectory. A heaviness hung in the air. Chris was used to feeling different energies in these old houses, but this energy made him feel as if something was watching his every move, sizing him up. He decided that he didn't like this place.

He left the front door open. The natural light made him feel better. Of course, it made sense that he felt judged here. He'd stopped attending church services decades ago, not to mention his recent divorce. Frankly, there was a lot about his life that didn't line up with what he'd learned in Sunday school.

Unclipping a tape measure from his belt, Chris started on the third floor and worked his way down. Scribbling notes about measurements and room conditions as he went, he was soon lost in his task and making good time.

Chris was halfway through the rooms on the second floor when he heard a *thunk* in a room down the hall—probably an animal lurking about the house. It wasn't uncommon. Yet a shiver rushed down his spine, and the hair on his arms stood at attention.

A blast of cold overtook him, which felt especially out of place, given the heat of the summer day. Chris knew, without knowing how he knew, that it was not an animal. He closed his eyes and said a prayer that he was surprised he remembered.

Forgetting his measurements for a moment, he poked his head out from the bedroom doorway and looked down the hall—just in time to see a dark, shadowy figure move into the room at the far end. The figure was wearing a priest's robe.

There was no way he'd be going into that room. In fact, he was ready to be done. Gathering his courage, he ventured into the hallway and rushed down the stairs, refusing to look behind the closed door he'd just seen the figure disappear through.

The sunlight streaming through the front door calmed him, and he was drawn to stand in the middle of it. Taking a few deep breaths, the tension he'd been holding onto released.

Feeling revived, Chris moved around the main floor, quickly getting the measurements he needed. He came across a closed door that he knew must lead to the basement. Putting his hand on the doorknob, he wondered if he could find the courage to venture into the cellar. Breathing deeply, he pulled the door open. The wave of energy that rushed out at him caught him off guard, even though he'd almost been expecting it.

Without hesitating, he slammed the door shut and raced out through the front door. Thankful that the key was still in the lock, he jiggled it until the door was secured.

After hurrying down to the street, he stood in the sunlight for a minute, letting it chase away the chills and calm his nerves. When his breathing patterns were back to normal, he slipped a small notebook out of his pocket to see how many rooms were left to measure. There were several.

With a shrug, he put away his notebook. It didn't matter how many rooms were left. Someone else would have to do them—because he was never going to set foot in the Sedamsville Rectory again.

Lake Erie College
Painsville

Lake Erie College was originally founded as the Willoughby Female Seminary in 1845. Its mission was to provide women with a "thorough and complete" female education. Ahead of its time, it was the only women's college in the Western Reserve—and the first college to be established with a female president and an all-female faculty.

In 1859, with an enrollment of 211 students, it was destroyed by a fire. Instead of rebuilding in Willoughby, the school's leaders chose a new location 15 miles east in Painsville. The school reopened as the Lake Erie Female Seminary.

In the early history of the newly reopened school, a mascot was adopted. Tiberius, a beloved chocolate lab, belonged to the dean, Harriet Young. The loyal dog accompanied students to class, wandered the buildings, and comforted anyone who needed it.

After Tiberius's death, Harriet commissioned an iron statue of him to place on campus. It wasn't long before a tradition evolved: Students would seek out the statue and give its head a pat for luck before exams, presentations, and sporting events.

In 1985, Lake Erie College (as it came to be known) became co-ed when it merged with Garfield Senior College. Although the original Tiberius statue was stolen and the second destroyed, a replica of the original still sits on campus, promising good luck to anyone who pats its head.

* * *

April 13, 1957

Mary Jean propped open the dorm-room window a crack, letting in the fresh night air.

"Is it okay with you if the window is open a little?" she asked her roommate, Letty. "Nights like these always remind me of sleeping at my grandmother's farm."

Letty smiled. "Sure, I had a grandmother like that too. And you're right, it's a nice night."

"If it gets too cold, I promise to get up and close it." She settled into her bed, snuggled underneath her blankets, and drifted to sleep.

* * *

Still half asleep, Mary Jean heard Letty calling her name.

"Alright," she mumbled. "I'll close the window."

"No," snapped Letty. "It's not that. Do you hear it?"

Sharp barks carried into the room.

"It sounds like a dog," Letty continued. "It sounds like it's right outside our window."

Now fully awake, Mary Jean crawled out of bed and peered outside. "I don't see anything."

Letty crept out of bed to look. "Me neither, but I know I heard it."

"I heard it too," said Mary Jean.

They turned away from the window. The barks started again, this time louder.

Mary Jean pulled her coat off the hook and slipped on her boots.

"Where are you going?" asked Letty.

"To investigate," said Mary Jean.

Surprising herself, Letty slipped her arms into her own coat. She wasn't usually bold enough to break the rules, even if it just meant sneaking out past curfew for 2 minutes to find a dog.

When they reached the front door, they heard the dog's insistent barking again. Now it was whining too.

"We'll catch it now," said Mary Jean.

However, when they pushed open the door, nothing was there.

"I know we heard it," said Letty. "It had to be standing right here . . . ."

They both saw the flames at the same time, coming from a third-floor window.

"The building is on fire!" screamed Mary Jean.

"Come on," shouted Letty. "We have to get everyone out."

They ran into their burning dormitory and up the stairs. They ran down the hallway, with Letty pounding on the doors to the right and Mary Jean taking the doors on the left.

"Wake up!" Mary Jean shouted.

"Memorial Hall," shouted Letty, "it's on fire!"

Sleepy girls began poking their heads into the hallway. Within minutes, all 19 girls from Memorial Hall were gathered on the walk, watching their beloved dorm—and all of their belongings—burn in a fire.

To this day, credit for the lives saved goes in part to the beloved campus watchdog, Tiberius. He stayed as loyal to his students in death as he had in life.

Licking County Historic Jail
Newark

Opening in November of 1889, the Licking County Jail operated for almost 100 years, until it closed in 1987. The four-story brownstone structure housed men and women on separate floors. Throughout its years in operation, 22 people reportedly died there, including three sheriffs.

Between the collective energy that came from hard criminals in captivity together—fearing what their fates might hold as they awaited sentencing—and the number of unnatural deaths (including several deaths by suicide), it's no wonder that the Licking County Historic Jail is known as one of the most haunted locations in the state. Most inmates housed at the jail could be considered typical, as far as criminals go, but some left legacies so chilling that they live on in the lore that makes the old jail notorious.

* * *

July 8, 1910

Seventeen-year-old Carl Etherington sat on the cot in the 8x8-foot concrete cell on the second floor of the Licking County Jail. The young deputy marshal never imagined himself on this side of the bars. When he, along with a team of other officers, served a warrant at a saloon for breaking Prohibition laws, they were attacked by a mob of men, infuriated by the government's meddling into how they chose to pass their time.

As the officers tried to escape, Carl was captured. He shot at the bar owner in self-defense, killing him. He hadn't known that the man was a former Newark police officer. Badly beaten by the mob of men, Carl was arrested and thrown into this cell.

He touched his swollen eyelid, cringing at the pain. He had joined the force because he wanted to keep people safe. He wanted to do what was right by the letter of the law. But he also knew the dangers. He understood that not everyone appreciated the law or the men who enforced it.

He'd stayed in this cell overnight, listening to the shouts of a crowd that had gathered outside. The sounds of their rage made it impossible for him to sleep. He tried to block out the noise, praying things would calm down and he could return home. Surely a man of the law, acting in self-defense while carrying out his duties, would not remain imprisoned.

The voices were drowned out by great thuds as rioters began battering the door of the prison, determined to avenge the death of a local man they respected. The sounds grew louder, and soon the voices of angry men echoed through the corridors of the jail, their feet clomping against the concrete in quick, harsh beats.

Carl's heartbeat quickened. As the wave of rage grew closer, he realized they were coming for him. It didn't take long for a horde of men to arrive at the front of his cell, screaming at him.

Their words were lost in the chaos of those moments. They cried out for his death. They screamed for him to burn in hell. None of it made sense to him. He had only been doing his job. He worked in service to them and their families.

Suddenly, the men were in his cell, their fists raining down upon him, pummeling his already bruised-and-swollen body. They dragged him through the hallway, down the steps, and out the front door, where thousands had gathered in rageful protest.

Carl asked to speak, perhaps hoping to appeal to the moral sense of those who'd gathered. He was never given the chance. They were intent on killing him, and nothing he could say or do would stop them.

A man with a hammer ran to him and crushed his skull with one firm blow. Young Carl's limp body was dragged to a light pole down the street, where he was hanged for all to see. The broken body of a young public servant swayed at the end of a noose.

The mob's actions that day killed a second person too. Carl's father, overcome by grief, ended his life less than two years later.

* * *

March 2025

The tap of footsteps echoed off the walls as the small tour group walked up the steps to the fourth floor.

"Do you think we'll get some interaction from Carl tonight when we investigate?" Teresa asked. She had come to the jail with a few of her friends, hoping to capture some evidence of paranormal activity.

"Anything's possible, but we typically don't. Not from him directly anyway," Darrin, the tour guide, explained. "People often get sick or feel a sense of anxiety in his cell though. It's like the energy of that night is trapped there."

He waited for the last person to climb the final step before continuing. "This is where the female inmates were housed," Darrin said. He stopped in front of a cell. "Fifty-five-year-old Mae Vaner was put in this cell on July 13, 1953. The police brought her from the hospital, where she had had her stomach pumped after overdosing. It wasn't Mae's first visit to Licking County Jail. She was a troubled woman."

Before Darrin could finish his next sentence, a muffled female voice seemed to carry over his voice.

"Did anyone else hear that?" Teresa asked.

"Yes," another woman nodded. "Is someone else here?"

"No, ma'am, it's just us," Darrin said. "We get that a lot though—a voice that seems to object when I mention Mae's troubles. We can never tell for sure what's being said, but Mae doesn't like us talking about her run-ins with the law."

Teresa and her friends looked around the corridor, a mix of excitement and trepidation on their faces.

Darrin continued, "She was well-known to the staff here, between incidents of domestic violence and overdoses. Once she even put her fist through a window."

A low moan emanated over Darrin's words. The tourists' eyes widened as they looked around.

Ghostly Tales of Ohio

"There it is again," Teresa said, a shiver running down her spine.

Darrin simply nodded before going on. "When they picked her up at the hospital, she told the sheriff, 'If you take me to jail, I'll just kill myself.' But that was Mae—she was known to make idle threats, so no one took her seriously."

Darrin motioned toward the cell as he spoke. "Matron Marie Thompson brought her to this cell. At that time, inmates could smoke in their cells, so Mae had a lighter. After the matron walked away, Mae used that lighter to set herself on fire. The matron came back to find Mae fully engulfed in flames. She tried to stomp the flames out, but it was too late."

The group fell silent. Everyone listened for more disembodied voices but heard none. The visitors took turns walking into the cell where poor, troubled Mae ended her life. Teresa could almost feel the heaviness of Mae's despair, as if the energy of her final moments was embedded in the concrete, the weight of her screams still hanging in the air decades later.

Teresa felt a pang of sadness; the way Mae had died was horrific. She thought of Mae's soul listening as her story was shared, time after time.

Those who visit the old jail might also experience sounds of slamming cell doors and disembodied screams. Videos and photographs have captured images of shadow figures lurking through the darkened corridors. Some guests have reported a general sense of dread, cold spots, and even being touched by unseen hands. Apparently, some lost souls are still there, awaiting their final judgement.

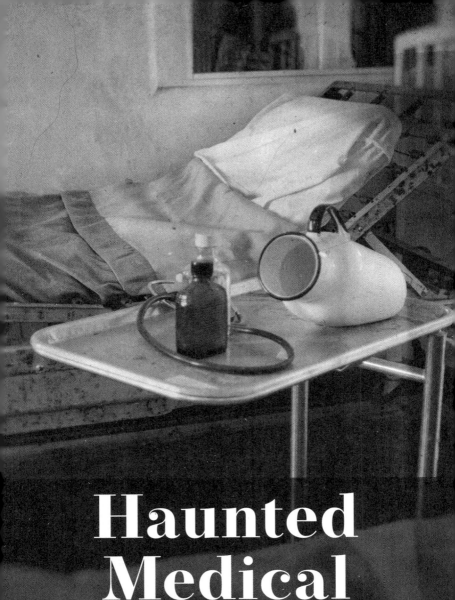

Haunted Medical Facilities

Molly Stark Sanatorium
Louisville

In the early 1900s, tuberculosis was rampant in the United States. With antibiotics still a long way off, the best method of containing this highly contagious disease was to isolate those who contracted it.

In August of 1929, the Molly Stark Sanatorium, named after the colonial wife of General John Stark, who served as a nurse during the Revolutionary War, opened its doors to provide treatment for those suffering from tuberculosis. With several balconies, verandas, and wide windows, the facility promised plenty of sunlight and fresh air.

After antibiotics entered the marketplace, the sanitorium evolved into a hospital in 1956. It was later used as a recovery center for those battling substance abuse, as well as a home for the elderly. Due to financial issues, the facility was ultimately closed to patients in 1995.

In 2009, the Stark County park board purchased the property for $1. In 2015, a fence was erected to prohibit paranormal enthusiasts and urban explorers from trespassing in the extremely unsafe building, which is infested with asbestos that has been disturbed by arson and water damage. No one is given permission to enter the building.

* * *

October 2000

Sheriff Swanson gathered deputies McDaniels and Freeman. They had been tasked with exploring the former sanitorium for any furniture or other items that could be sold at the upcoming county auction. They brought a small group of inmates with them to help move whatever items they found.

"We stay together," the sheriff explained to his deputies before they got the inmates out of the van. "I don't want anyone wandering off alone."

"I wouldn't think of it," said Freeman. "I've heard stories about this place."

"Like what?" asked McDaniels.

"The S.W.A.T. team was training here not long ago. One guy saw a man staring at them from a window as they arrived. Once they were inside, a man in a brown suit appeared from out of nowhere and ran down a corridor. When they chased after him, he disappeared into nothing."

Sheriff Swanson added, "I may have heard a story or two myself. Along with a handful of claims about footsteps, people mentioned that they heard the elevators moving."

"Old elevators can easily short-circuit, right?" asked McDaniels.

"Not if they don't have an elevator in them anymore," said the sheriff.

The deputies remained quiet, letting that sink in.

The sheriff continued, "The chief of police stayed overnight a couple of times. His dog would howl and whine at something in the hallway. No one could say why."

"Okay, I agree that we should stick together," said Freeman, practically cutting off the sheriff. "I don't want to know what was in the hallway."

Sheriff Swanson laughed and went to get the inmates out of the van.

* * *

Max looked up at the imposing structure from his window in the police van. He and a few other inmates had been chosen to help gather furniture from inside. He had been excited about the idea of a field trip, happy to be selected for a job that would take him away from the monotonous daily life of an inmate, even for just a couple of hours. Now he wasn't so sure.

He couldn't explain it, but he felt like the building was watching him—or maybe it was someone in the building who was watching. He shook away the thought. No one had occupied this part of the building for decades. His eyes scanned the windows of the top floor. He was torn between wanting to find an explanation for the feeling and not wanting to know if something was in there.

And then he saw it: a man's face in the middle window of the top floor. The man was staring back at him. Max looked around the van to see if anyone else saw it, but no one was paying attention. Max

Ghostly Tales of Ohio

wasn't about to say anything. He'd survived this long by keeping his head down and his mind on the task in front of him.

The van door slid open, and Sheriff Swanson instructed them to get out.

"This is the part where I remind you all that you need to be on your best behavior."

The inmates nodded. They were all mere weeks away from their parole hearings. No one was going to risk doing anything that would ruin their chances of getting paroled.

The sheriff removed their cuffs, and they walked to a side door of the impressive building.

"We're looking for anything that's salvageable to sell at the county auction," said Sheriff Swanson. "And we're all sticking together."

Max nodded, feeling better. There was safety in numbers.

They were about an hour into their task and had already moved through several rooms on the first floor. Anything of value was placed in the hallway to be collected later. At first, the abandoned hospital carts, empty metal bed frames, and vacant lounge chairs were startling—especially when Max realized that no one had sat in these chairs or slept in these beds since before he was born. But he had gotten used to seeing the things, layered with dust and debris from the crumbling walls and ceilings.

He nearly forgot about the face he'd seen, watching him from the upper window—until he heard a massive screech, like metal scraping against the floor, coming from the level above them. There was no questioning whether anyone else had heard it. Everyone, inmates and deputies alike, stopped in their tracks.

Shivers danced along the back of Max's neck, and he knew, without a doubt, that it was somehow connected to the face he had seen in the window.

"Alright," said the sheriff. "I suppose we should check that out."

"We?" asked an inmate.

Max was impressed that he'd found the courage to ask the single-word question that was burning in his own mind.

"We're sticking together, remember?" said the sheriff. He led them out the door, hand on his holster.

The deputies waited for the inmates to follow, then brought up the rear, their hands also at the ready near their weapons. Max felt a strange sense of comfort, knowing they were armed—yet not sure what a gun would do to save them from a ghost.

When they got to the second floor, they entered a room that seemed to be the source of the noise. Max could already feel that this room was different. Its energy was . . . off. His shivers were back. This time, they ran all the way down his back, across his arms, and down his legs, making it difficult to keep putting one foot in front of the other.

The inmate next to him gasped audibly, and Max saw it too: The bed had been dragged to the middle of the room, leaving fresh tracks through the dust on the floor.

The visible, tangible evidence validated what Max had been feeling all along. This building hid something in its shadows: restless souls, lingering in the empty rooms, crying out to be remembered.

The Willoughby Medical Facility
Willoughby

By 1820, Dr. John Henderson and Dr. George Card had settled into a town not far from the edge of Lake Erie in the northeast corner of the state. The doctors, both of whom had studied at the Fairfield Medical College in New York, planned to open their own medical school. They officially renamed the town "Willoughby" after the president of their alma mater, with hopes of enticing him to become the head of their school. However, Dr. Willoughby politely declined, citing his wife's poor health.

Nevertheless, in 1834, the Willoughby University of Lake Erie was granted a charter by the Ohio legislature. Dr. John C. Bennett became the school's first president. With a town and a school named after a doctor from New York who had never even been to Ohio, the school set out on its mission to train doctors.

* * *

Summer 1845

Eli Tarbell was too weak to open his eyes, but he could feel his wife's presence beside him. The heat from the day, combined with the heat from his fever, was simply too much. He heard the familiar drip of water into the basin as his wife wrung out the cloth she'd been using to dab the sweat from his brow.

Three weeks earlier, he'd become too ill to get out of bed. Typhoid fever, the doctors had declared. Since then, Eli had grown weaker by the day.

As the cold cloth touched his forehead, a shiver went down his spine. He gathered as much strength as he could muster and grabbed his wife's hand. He gripped it, using her strength to gather his own. After several minutes, he forced himself to open his eyes.

Tears streamed down his wife's face.

He stared into her steel-blue eyes. "I . . . I . . .," he stammered.

"Hush now," she whispered. "You need your strength." But her voice cracked, telling Eli that she knew what he knew.

He smiled weakly. "I love you, old girl. You are my one and only . . ."

". . . forever and always," she finished, like she always did.

Their familiar exchange had gone on for decades. Eli couldn't remember when they had started saying it.

"Be strong," he whispered.

She leaned over and lay her head on his chest. He could feel her body shake with sobs. Eli patted her gray head. If they had learned anything through the years, it was that life wasn't easy. But they had made a good go of it, together.

"It was good," he whispered, "because of you." Eli exhaled, breathing his last breath.

* * *

Eli's widow went through the next three days in a grief-stricken daze. Arrangements were made, and the funeral happened fast. With the sweltering Ohio heatwave, there was no time to waste.

She sat on the front porch, sipping from a glass of whiskey. Her husband wasn't much of a drinker, but he always kept a bottle on hand. "For emergencies," he'd always said. She decided this qualified.

Today had been about trying to put her house back together—alone. An overwhelming loneliness loomed, like an uninvited guest at a party.

How am I ever going to do this? she wondered for the millionth time. She didn't have any more tears left to cry.

The worry of the past several weeks, along with the stress of the past three days, had taken its toll. Breathing in the humid air, she was overwhelmed with exhaustion. She finished her drink and went into the house. Not bothering to undress, she fell into bed and settled into a deep sleep.

The dream began with everything just as she'd lived it: the wake in the parlor, the service, the burial—everything. But then Eli was there. She could feel his essence. He was wearing his Sunday best, just as he'd been wearing in his coffin.

Eli held up his arm for her to see. Everything below the elbow was completely gone.

"They cut it off and took it!" he shouted, his voice filled with rage.

The scene changed. Suddenly, she was in a classroom in the medical college. Students were gathered around, watching, as her husband's body was carved apart.

She sat upright in bed, dripping with sweat. A chill crept through her, one that shouldn't be possible on such a hot night.

A calm, familiar presence washed over her, and she knew that she wasn't alone. Eli had shown her what was happening to him.

"Make them stop," he whispered, and then he faded to nothing.

She squeezed her eyes shut, willing him to come back. She wanted to feel him beside her again, one more time.

The next morning, Eli's widow awoke with renewed strength. She went first to her daughter's house. Then, together, they went to the cemetery. The five white flowers she had left behind were mangled and scattered—proof that the grave had been disturbed.

The two women marched through town, gathering neighbors, telling anyone who would listen about her dream and Eli's disturbed grave. She expected people to call her crazy, but they didn't. Everyone believed her. After all, it was exactly what many in town had feared when they opened the medical college in the first place.

The mob stormed the college and demanded justice. They wanted to know where Eli was. Just as his wife had feared, his body was found in parts.

The college never recovered from the scandal, and its doors closed in 1847. However, it didn't go out of business. It simply relocated, becoming the Starling Medical College in Columbus.

Decades later, body snatchers were still doing steady business, fueled by the need for human specimens for medical students to study. In 1878, *The New York Times* published a chilling exposé on the body-snatching industry. The story outlined how grave robbers scoured funeral notices for prime candidates. Often, doctors would accompany the robbers on their missions, making sure they got what they needed. In the account, one of the corpses had belonged to a butcher. A doctor who was interviewed recounted, quite casually, that he'd bought meat from the man many times—but now, he was the one who'd be selling the man for meat.

* * *

As ghost stories have proven, time and again, sometimes the dead don't rest peacefully—for good reason. In the case of Eli Tarbell, he came back to expose a sinister grave-robbing ring. A lot of credit must go to his widow, who believed his message from beyond the grave, took up the cause, and did everything she could to help him rest in peace.

The Ridges
Athens

Originally known as the Athens Lunatic Asylum, the Ridges focused on treating people with psychiatric disabilities through kindness, daily routines, and the beauty of nature and the arts. The first patient was welcomed to the 544-bed facility in 1874.

What began as a single structure became a complex of 78 buildings on roughly 700 acres of land. It boasted 60 acres of parklike spaces, including an array of trees and flowers, walking paths, four ponds, and a waterfall. The location was intentionally designed to improve patients' emotional well-being through nature.

By the 1950s, around 1,800 patients were cared for at the facility. During these years, Dr. Walter Freeman made annual visits to perform hundreds of lobotomies. These were dark days for mental healthcare. Freeman traveled across the US, "treating" more than 3,400 patients, leaving hundreds dead and many others disabled.

* * *

December 1, 1978

Margaret Shilling was a creature of habit. Every morning, staff and patients could count on seeing her, standing at the top of the stairs, a smile and a wave for anyone who passed by. By all accounts, the 53-year-old woman was quiet and kept to herself, but her kindness emanated from that perch on the landing.

"Good morning, Margaret," Nancy said as she stepped across the landing and descended the steps.

Margaret's eyes lit up as she smiled in response. Nancy hit the bottom step and turned to see Margaret waving. Nancy waved back before hurrying on her way. It was an unremarkable interaction, just another day filled with routines and quirks that came with the patients.

* * *

December 2, 1978

Nancy moved quickly to get through her morning work. She walked to the stairs and started her descent. She stopped halfway down and peered over her shoulder. There was no one standing at the top to smile and wave.

"Where's Margaret?" she wondered aloud.

Nancy's coworker Kathleen paused at the bottom of the steps. "She's probably off enjoying the view from the windows," she said with a shrug before hurrying on her way.

The view from upstairs was breathtaking, overlooking the landscaped grounds. In the winter months, many patients looked out from there with a longing for warmer weather, when they could spend their days lounging under the sprawling branches of the old trees.

Kathleen was probably right. Margaret had open privileges, with free rein to roam the facility as she wished. Nancy made a note to keep an eye out for her.

Several hours later, as residents left the dining room to go about their evening routines, Nancy stood at the bottom of the stairs, looking up at the spot where she'd last seen Margaret the day before.

"She wasn't at dinner," she said to the managing nurse. "Something's wrong."

It wasn't long before most of the staff was spread throughout the 700,000-square-foot building, looking for Margaret. The search moved outside to the grounds, but dark shadows of night made it difficult.

The next morning, the Athens police conducted an organized search of the property. They checked each outbuilding and scoured inside, from the basement to the attic.

"She must have left," an officer declared to the managing nurse.

"That doesn't make sense," Nancy said.

"We've looked everywhere," Kathleen replied. "If she were here, we would have found her."

* * *

January 11, 1979

The maintenance worker walked up the narrow staircase of the tower, shivering from the chilly air. This portion of the asylum had been closed off from the rest of the building. There was no heat to combat the frigid winter winds blowing against the bowed walls of windows that made the tower so bright.

He entered the top floor. For a moment, it was just another abandoned room in the century-old building—

chipped paint, cracked plaster, and dust-covered concrete floors. But he quickly realized something was wrong.

Over near the windows, a nude female body lay motionless. Sunlight shone in like a macabre spotlight on the prone, decomposing corpse. Her clothes were neatly folded beside her. Margaret Shilling had been found.

* * *

Fall 2022

Sean was just wrapping up his shift in the lab. Most of the students had long since left. His friend Jackie was the last to remain, her book open on a table as she studied, waiting to walk to their dormitory together.

"Give me 5 minutes to tidy up," Sean said.

"Sounds good," Jackie replied, not looking up from her book.

Not far away, the hinges of a door creaked before it slammed shut. The sound pulled Jackie from her book. She and Sean looked toward the open door, expecting to see someone come in. But there was no sound of approaching footsteps.

The local community had been thrilled that Ohio University took over the place after it closed in 1993, saving the beloved campus from demolition. Given that the building—now known as the Ridges—was roughly 150 years old, creaks came with the territory—but knowing it once served as a psychiatric hospital sometimes made those creaks seem creepy.

Sean returned his attention to getting the lab cleaned and ready for tomorrow. At last, he heard the distinct sound of footsteps—but not where he expected them to be. They were coming from another room. They were slow, soft, and followed by a whimper.

Sean's eyes widened. Jackie put her book down and moved beside him. They stood in silence, listening to what sounded like someone crying.

"Could it be coming from the room where the stain is?" Jackie asked, her voice barely a whisper.

Sean nodded, knowing the room wasn't far away. He had seen the stain once before. His curiosity got to him one afternoon when he was talking to another grad student about the tragic legend of Margaret Shilling. He and the other student found the room unlocked, so they let themselves in.

Margaret had died from natural causes, specifically heart failure likely brought on by hypothermia. The stain left behind—apparently from fluids that seeped out while the body decomposed—could not be removed.

Sean remembered it as the eeriest thing he had ever seen, the perfect outline of Margaret's body like a stamp on the gray concrete.

There were more shuffling footsteps, followed by what sounded like a door being pounded on and more whimpering. Sean had heard stories of the hauntings at the Ridges. Rattling door handles, disembodied screams, and disappearing specters were among the reported activity.

Without a word, he and Jackie grabbed their belongings and rushed out of the room. They hurried outside and walked quickly away, still not speaking. When they'd put a safe distance between themselves and the building, they stopped, looked at one another, then glanced toward the window of the room where Margaret had left her eternal mark.

The dark shape of a woman—more like a shadow than flesh and bone—looked out, watching them.

Was Margaret's spirit still in the place where she'd been trapped so long ago, waiting for someone to find her? The thought sent shivers down Sean's spine. He and Jackie hustled away, certain that Margaret's watchful eyes were on them the entire way.

Haunted Hotels & Historic Businesses

Buxton Inn
Granville

January 1946

Ethel "Bonnie" Bounell walked slowly through the lobby, pausing once to straighten a floral arrangement in a vase. Her adopted kitten, Major Buxton, purred as Bonnie made sure each flower was spread out just so. A former opera singer, Bonnie found peace in this new phase of her life, as the owner of the Buxton Inn.

Her husband, a prominent attorney, had passed away in 1933. Bonnie purchased the old inn (in need of some repairs) the following year. She managed the place alongside her dearest friend, Nell Schoeller, who oversaw the kitchen. The women restored the inn to its former glory and made it their home.

Bonnie understood that it was a treasured piece of history, and she was honored to be its caretaker. Built in 1812 as a stagecoach stop, it had been the last place for travelers to rest for an evening as they made their way to Columbus. It also served as part of the Underground Railroad. A hidden door leading to a secret room could still be found behind the bar on the second floor.

She smoothed the skirt of her blue dress as she walked out of the lobby, past the main staircase, and into the dining room. Upon entering, she glimpsed someone out of the corner of her eye: a man in a dark suit, wearing a top hat, warming his hands by the fire.

The image was quick but clear. She turned to look directly at him, but the spot was empty—as she expected. It was just another fleeting glimpse of her kitten's namesake, Major Horton Buxton, who had owned the inn from 1865 until his death in 1902.

It was common knowledge that the Buxton Inn was haunted. Bonnie could understand how a soul might want to stop in to see this special place. It had been a destination of comfort for so many. Presidents, including Abraham Lincoln, and other renowned businessmen, such as Bonnie's friends Harvey Firestone and Henry Ford, had spent time at the inn. For all Bonnie knew, her spirit might pop in long after her body had been laid to rest. She couldn't help but smile at the thought. Her cat purred again. Maybe they'd both stick around.

* * *

Mid-1980s

It had been a long day, and Janis was looking forward to falling asleep in a warm bed. The work retreat was a nice switch from the hustle of managing all the other nurses at her hospital. Several of her colleagues were staying at the Buxton Inn too.

Janis was glad she'd chosen this over a chain hotel. The place had so much historic charm, from the old metal lock on the front door to the unique alternating pattern of dark walnut and light chestnut wood planks on the lobby floor—details that made the inn feel uniquely old and new at the same time. Janis felt as if she were stepping into history the moment she walked through the front door.

She shut the door of Room 7 and set her purse on the antique desk. Flipping through her day planner, she eyed tomorrow's itinerary before closing the book and placing it beside her purse.

As she settled into bed, she pulled up the blankets and melted into the warmth of the cozy room. She breathed in the room's pleasant smell of gardenias. After she finally tumbled into a restless slumber, she was startled awake, as if something had pulled her from sleep. The room was so thick with darkness that Janis could hardly see the nightstand beside the bed. She listened intently, sensing that a noise had awakened her.

Ffffft.

Something soft, almost indiscernible seemed to move.

Ffffft.

Her heartbeat quickened as the familiarity of the sound clicked in her mind. Someone was flipping through the pages of the planner she'd left on the desk. Janis held her breath as she listened until the sound stopped. Her eyes slowly adjusted to the darkness of the room, and she looked for someone near the desk. No one was there.

The door to her room opened with a soft squeak, and an older woman in white walked in. For a moment,

Janis's mind rationalized that one of her coworkers had entered, but it was the middle of the night. Why would any of them come into her room?

I'm dreaming, she thought.

The woman walked across the room and settled into the chair near the bed. Janis knew the woman shouldn't be there, but there was something oddly comforting about her.

"You can't sleep, can you?" the woman asked, her voice like a whisper in Janis's ear.

"No," Janis replied.

Somehow, with the woman quietly watching over her, Janis did slip back to sleep.

* * *

"Good morning, Janis," said Marie, one of her colleagues, as she entered the lobby.

Janis had awakened early, her mind replaying the odd dream she'd had about the woman in her room—except she couldn't convince herself it was a dream.

Janis replied. "I had the strangest dream last night."

The front-desk clerk listened with the other nurses, as Janis explained what had happened.

"Can you describe what the woman looked like?" the clerk asked.

"She had dark, curly hair and a soft face with round cheeks. She was pretty, and she was wearing a dress with billowed sleeves that seemed like something from another era."

"Just a minute," the clerk said. He dipped behind the desk and reemerged with a photo album. Thumbing through the pages, he stopped at one with a newspaper clipping slipped behind the protective plastic sheath.

"Oh my gosh," Janis said, her voice shrill. "That's her!"

"That's Bonnie Bounell," the clerk noted. "She owned the inn between 1934 and 1960. You're not the first person to see her."

"I heard this place was haunted," Marie said, her eyes wide. "But I can't believe you saw a ghost."

Janis couldn't believe it either, but as she looked at the woman, smiling at her from the old news clipping, she couldn't deny that it was the same woman who had visited her the night before.

* * *

In addition to Bonnie, ghostly presences at the Buxton Inn are said to include the original owner, Orrin Granger, and Major Horton Buxton, who renamed the inn to bear his name. The spirit of a young child, known as the "Tavern Boy," is believed to have been a passenger on a stagecoach who became ill, was quarantined in the basement, and died there. Even Bonnie's beloved cat, Major Buxton, continues to charm guests from beyond the grave.

It's an eclectic mix of souls, spanning decades, who've decided to stop by the place that brought them so much joy. Visitors might hear their disembodied footsteps walking through the hallways or feel the unmistakable nudge of a cat pressing against their ankles. They might even see a full-body apparition when they least expect it.

The Lafayette Hotel
Marietta

In 1892, the Bellevue Hotel was constructed on a corner of land where the Muskingum River joined the Ohio River. On April 26, 1916, a fire ravaged the building, destroying the hotel. The Lafayette Hotel was built on the same location and was named after Marquis de Lafayette, who visited the city in 1825. Lafayette was a revered hero of the American Revolution and was considered Marietta's first official tourist. A plaque was placed near the hotel to commemorate the spot where Lafayette first arrived.

The historic hotel—especially the third floor—is notoriously haunted. Most of the paranormal activity seems to come from spirits that are curious, playful, and mischievous, rather than malicious or scary.

* * *

Fall 2015

Sam ordered a bacon cheeseburger with fries to go and then wandered over to a vintage painting that featured a riverboat and riverfront scene. He was glad to be done with his presentation from earlier that morning, even thought it had gone very well. He was grateful that he could enjoy the rest of the conference without that chore hanging over his head.

He took the lunch to his third-floor room and set the Styrofoam box on the coffee table. The smell of bacon overpowered the room. Despite an audible rumble that came from his stomach, Sam remembered how many hands he'd shaken downstairs and ducked into the bathroom to wash up.

When he returned less than a minute later, he froze. The box was gone.

His brain struggled to find an explanation. Sam glanced at the deadbolt on the door; it was locked. The smell of bacon still lingered, but his burger was nowhere in the room.

Confused, Sam went back down to the bar.

"Can I get you something else to eat or drink, sir?" asked the bartender.

Sam looked down, a little overwhelmed with embarrassment. "Uh, I somehow lost my burger and need to order another."

The bartender raised an eyebrow but moved to the register to ring in the new food order.

"I really don't know how to explain it," said Sam. "I went up to my room and set the lunch on the coffee table. I turned around for just a minute, and then it was gone."

The bartender nodded with a slight grin. "You're on the third floor, right?"

"Yeah," said Sam. "Why?"

"If something nutty is going to happen, it's usually on the third floor. The housekeepers have things go missing all the time, only to turn up again later. We've got quite a trickster up there."

"Do you mean a ghost?" Sam whispered. He wasn't sure he believed in ghosts.

"Don't worry. It's never anything bad. You want this burger to go too?"

"No," said Sam, "I'd better eat it right here."

When his food arrived, Sam ate in silence, still trying to figure out what could have happened to his first order. He hated to admit it, but it seemed that the only possible explanation was something paranormal.

* * *

The following day, Sam stopped at his room before lunch. As he fished his key out from his pocket, the smell of bacon wafted into the hallway. He wondered if someone else was about to fall victim to the same ghostly prank.

When he opened the door, he was surprised that the smell grew stronger. There, on the coffee table, was yesterday's Styrofoam container, exactly where he'd set it before it disappeared.

He grabbed the white box and looked inside. Sure enough, it was a bacon cheeseburger and a pile of fries.

"What in the world?"

He took it down to the bar, but a different bartender was working.

"Look," he said anyway, handing the box to the bartender. "I just found it in my room."

She peeked inside the box. "A bacon cheeseburger and fries?" she asked, confused.

"It's the one I ordered yesterday. It disappeared when I went to wash my hands."

"Oh, yeah," she said. "I heard about that."

"Is someone messing with me?" he asked. "Did someone put this in there?"

"I don't think so," she said. "We just opened for lunch, and I haven't taken any to-go orders. We're out of bacon too. Your box couldn't have come from this kitchen today."

"Are you sure?" he asked.

"That's Jack's handwriting on the box," she said, pointing to the scrawl in the corner. "He's not even here today."

Sam was quiet. Reluctantly, he handed her the container. "Can you toss this for me?"

She nodded. "Yeah. And how about I pour you a beer?"

Sam nodded. "Thanks."

He settled himself onto the barstool and tried to think about the quantum physics of a burger reappearing out of thin air. He would probably spend the rest of his life wondering about it.

Park Hotel
Put-in-Bay

Built in 1873, the hotel initially hosted passengers of steamships crossing Lake Erie. Early in the hotel's history, there were three reported deaths. The first was believed to have been owner George F. Schmidt (or possibly "Smith"), who allegedly died after shooting himself. A similar suicide occurred not long after the first, when a guest returned from an evening of heavy drinking and assigned himself the same fate. The third death, occurring around 1900, was that of a woman, known only as "the Governess." Her foot reportedly became entangled in her hoop skirt as she walked down the steps, causing her to tumble and break her neck.

With more than 150 years of history and many thousands of visitors, it's no surprise that the hotel is one of the most haunted locations in Ohio. It encapsulated both joy and sorrow as lives were lived and lost within its walls—and the hotel has never forgotten them.

* * *

September 2010

The hotel staff was on its annual road trip, a Park Hotel tradition to celebrate the end of another visitor season on South Bass Island. Phil stayed back to get some maintenance work done. On this morning, he had the place to himself.

Growing up in Put-in-Bay, he knew the hotel was special. His childhood friend Mike had lived in the hotel with his family, who owned it. Now Mike was running the operation and had happily given Phil a job as maintenance manager.

Phil's plan today was to clean all the AC units. The units were about to sit idle for several months, now that summer was racing toward fall. He settled into Room 21 and got to work.

As he was about to finish, ready to slide the unit back into the wall, he heard a man's voice behind him. "Are you about done?"

"I will be soon," Phil replied without looking back, thinking that Mike must have returned to the hotel.

After getting the unit into place, Phil walked out of the room and stopped at the top of the steps. "Hey, Mike, what do you need?" he hollered.

There was no response. Mike must have found something else to do.

Phil continued cleaning the AC units. When he finished, he headed down to Mike's office and found him working at his desk.

"What did you need earlier?" asked Phil.

"What do you mean?" replied Mike.

"When you were upstairs and asked if I was about done. Did you need help with something?"

Ghostly Tales of Ohio

Mike replied, "I just walked in the door a few minutes ago. I haven't been upstairs."

Someone had been; Phil was sure of it. But if it hadn't been Mike, it couldn't have been anyone else. The entire place was locked up.

Phil had heard stories of the hotel being haunted. He even recalled hanging out there as a kid, closing the same door repeatedly after it opened several times on its own. At the time, he and Mike never thought twice about it. Now, he realized that locked doors shouldn't open on their own.

* * *

By January of the following year, Phil had stepped in as hotel manager. He moved into the apartment on the first floor and reported hearing footsteps on the upper levels when the place was otherwise empty. He also noticed the smell of pipe tobacco in the dining room, as well as doors opening and closing on their own.

One winter evening, while the hotel was closed for the season, Phil heard footsteps rushing down the stairs, followed by someone hurrying across the lobby and leaving through the front door. However, the hotel staff blocked off the staircase with a temporary wall during winter to conserve energy. It was physically impossible for anyone to travel down the steps and into the lobby, due to the wall. Yet he heard it happen time and again.

Over the years, ghostly apparitions of Victorian-era men and women have been reported throughout the hotel by guests and staff, including what is suspected to be the spirit of the Governess, who seems particularly protective of children. Phantom voices, eerie strains of ballroom music, and spectral figures make the Park Hotel a paranormal hot spot worthy of its notoriety.

Punderson Manor
Newbury Township

Punderson Manor rises along the edge of Punderson Lake in picturesque Punderson State Park. Construction of the private residence began in the late 1920s, but when the stock market crashed in 1929, the project was abandoned.

Some 20 years later, the manor was completed, and the state of Ohio purchased it. The area was developed into a state park, and the manor became a lodge. Not long after that, visitors began reporting mysterious activities, from doors opening and closing on their own to the sound of children's laughter when no children were present.

One park ranger heard the disembodied laughter of a woman as he made his way up the main staircase. When he entered the hallway above, he was struck by a blast of frigid air that seemed to travel down the corridor. The laughter stopped abruptly, leaving the ranger bewildered.

Some visitors have reported being touched by unseen hands. One woman even claimed to be held down on her bed by what felt like multiple entities. Perhaps the most disturbing legend involves a lumberjack, a noose, and a late-night vision that was shared by three employees.

* * *

1979

Pat, Alex, and Terry were well into their overnight shift at the lodge's front desk, without much to do. Guests had long since retired to their rooms.

"I'm sure the fresh brew of coffee is ready," Alex said. "Let's stretch our legs and grab a cup."

"One of us should stay at the desk," Terry said.

Alex replied, "It's 3 a.m. Who's going to need something at this time of night?"

The trio made their way to the kitchen and filled their cups. As they walked into the room that would later become the lounge, they were stunned to see the figure of a man, dangling from the rafters.

The employees froze in their tracks.

"Do you see that?" Terry asked.

"Yes," Pat whispered. "He looks like a lumberjack."

A long rope, wrapped around the man's neck, extended toward the ceiling, fading just before it reached the rafters. That point of disconnection made it clear that this wasn't a guest in need of medical assistance. It was a spirit from the past.

For a while they stood in silence, transfixed by the image. Eventually, one of them sat down, and the others followed suit. For 3 hours, the employees watched the man slowly spinning at the bottom of that rope.

His body appeared as solid as their own until light from the morning sunrise began to filter through the windows. It was then that his form began to fade. Before long, the specter was gone, leaving the three witnesses dumbfounded, still staring in awe at the empty place where the man once hung.

* * *

The question as to why Punderson Manor is haunted is as mysterious as the hauntings themselves. As more ghostly experiences are reported, speculation becomes embedded in the legend of the place. Myth and reality become blurred, leaving us with unfounded tales, like that of the original property owner, Lemuel Punderson, rowing to the center of the lake in a bathtub in 1822, pulling the plug, and sinking to his death. In reality, the man passed away from complications caused by malaria.

Who haunts Punderson Manor—and why? The questions may remain unanswered forever.

The Golden Lamb
Lebanon

In 1803, the state of Ohio issued a license to Jonas Seaman, so he could open a public house of entertainment. His business operated out of a log cabin and became a stopping point for the stagecoach line. In 1815, the business—which eventually became known as the Golden Lamb Inn—moved to its current brick building.

In 1882, a little girl named Sarah Stubbs came to live at the Golden Lamb with her mother and baby sister. Her father had died, so they moved in with her uncle, Albert Stubbs, the manager of the hotel. Even though Sarah lived until the age of 79, she is said to haunt the hotel as a 5-year-old. She sometimes shows herself to children, and guests report hearing her laughter.

Other reported ghosts on the premises include Clement L. Vallandingham. The US Congressman died while staying at the Golden Lamb when he accidentally shot himself. His spirit is often accompanied by the strong smell of cigar smoke.

The state added the Golden Lamb Inn to the National Register of Historic Places in the 1970s, and it has the honor of being Ohio's oldest continuously operating business.

* * *

Winter 2012

"Mama, how much longer?" young James whined, stretching out the last word for dramatic effect.

"Not much longer," said his mother, although she wasn't sure. It had been her response the last three times he'd asked. She looked around the lobby at the other couples who waited, realizing that she and her husband were the only ones with a child.

"We shouldn't have gone out for dinner tonight," she whispered to her husband.

Two weeks before Christmas, it seemed like everyone in town had the same idea.

He shrugged. "They have prime rib tonight. I'm sure it will just be another minute. I'll check."

"Mama?" James tugged on his mother's sleeve. "Is it okay if I go play with the little girl over there?" he asked.

"What little girl?" she replied, looking around.

"The one in the white dress, on the stairs."

She looked at the stairs. "There's no one there. Where is she now?"

"Don't you see her? She's waving at me to come."

Her husband returned. "They're ready for us."

"Oh, good," she said, relieved. "Let's go, James."

James waved at the empty staircase. His mother glanced over her shoulder, wondering what her son could see that she couldn't.

* * *

Ghostly Tales of Ohio

Sometimes, ghosts haunt a location because their soul is stuck. Other times, spirits return to a place at the age they were when they lived there. If little Sarah Stubbs is lingering at the Golden Lamb as a 5-year-old—even though she died in old age—perhaps she is revisiting a time in her life that brought her security after the traumatic death of her father. Or as others have suggested, maybe a sliver of her soul is stuck at the hotel because of the trauma she experienced at that time in her life. Or perhaps the little ghost is a different child altogether. These are the sorts of questions that keep paranormal investigators searching for answers, hoping to solve the ghostly mysteries that remain.

The Akron Civic Theater
Akron

In 1929, the Akron community gained what became known as the "Jewel on Main Street." Originally named the Loews Theater after its owner, Marcus Loew, the iconic Akron Civic Theater later became a historic landmark. It's also haunted.

A young man named Paul Steeg helped to open the theater in 1929 and worked there until his death in 1972. He reportedly talked about how he would never leave the theater. Some believe that he kept his promise even after death.

A well-dressed gentleman in period clothes is often seen sitting in the upper balcony. In addition, Fred, a former janitor, is described as a helpful spirit. He regularly helps keep patrons in line, and he supposedly doesn't like it when the bathrooms get messy. He is known as a ghost that has no tolerance for disrespect.

Prior to the opening of the theater, the nearby Ohio and Erie Canal was in use, carrying freight traffic until 1861. It is believed that a young woman threw herself into the canal and died. The theater was built over the spot where this is said to have happened. The young woman allegedly haunts Lock 3 and is often seen walking along the canal. Witnesses have reported that, once she is seen, she will disappear into the tunnel under the theater. Others have heard uncontrollable weeping, without being able to identify a source. Some guests have noted that she will leave a trail of wet footprints before she disappears.

* * *

Summer 2012

Adam punched the button at the crosswalk to change the light. There were only a few cars around, so crossing against the light would have been easy. But on a Saturday night, when theatergoers and restaurant patrons were heading for home, it was better not to take chances.

As he turned the corner onto Main Street, Adam tried not to think about how late he'd gotten off his shift as a bartender—or how early he'd have to be back in the morning to greet the brunch crowd. He hated back-to-back shifts like that, but those shifts were always lucrative and coveted, so he could hardly complain.

His thoughts were interrupted when he heard a woman's voice shout, "No, get away from me."

Up ahead, he saw a woman outside the Civic Theater. A man had her by the arms, and he was trying to drag her. Adam broke into a run and was about to shout—when a ghostly figure appeared next to the woman. The spectral presence grew, as if it were intentionally making itself bigger.

The man let go of the woman. The spirit stepped between the attacker and his victim, as if to protect her. The man turned and ran, and the spirit disappeared.

Adam hurried to the woman. "Are you okay?" he asked.

"Yeah, I . . . think so," she stammered, shaking.

She was wearing a white blouse and black pants, the tell-tale uniform of a server. Adam assumed she was just getting off her restaurant shift, like he was.

"Did you see that?" she asked.

"What, him grabbing you?" asked Adam.

"No, the reason he let go."

"I did, but I don't believe it." Adam looked up at the marquee of the theater. "Maybe it's true what they say about this place."

"What's that?" she asked.

"The ghosts here are protective. They look out for people."

The woman was quiet.

"Should we call the police?" asked Adam.

She shook her head. "I wouldn't know how to explain what happened without sounding crazy."

Adam wanted to disagree, but he didn't press her. "Can I walk you to your car?" he asked.

"Sure, it's right there," she said, pointing to the side street.

When they reached her car, she fished the keys out of her pocket. "It was a ghost, right?" She looked straight at him, as if she could see the answer in his soul.

"Yes," said Adam. "I think so."

"Okay, I just needed to make sure."

Ghostly Tales of Ohio 73

He watched as she drove away. Adam knew what he'd seen, and he knew the stories about the Civic Theater and its ghosts. There was no doubt that one of them had helped to keep that woman safe.

* * *

As the Akron Civic Theater ghosts seem to prove, some spirits are watchful and protective. On that summer night, maybe Fred stood against the violence in front of his theater. Maybe the sad young woman was momentarily distracted from her own pain to prevent someone else's. Or maybe this attack victim had a powerful guardian angel who was there to protect her. Whatever the case may be, stories like this are evidence that, sometimes, spiritual forces want to help.

Haunted Houses & Mansions

Franklin Castle
Cleveland

Hannes and Luise Tiedemann purchased the home on Franklin Boulevard in 1865. In the first 16 years they lived there, they lost four of their six children. Needing a fresh start, they decided to tear down the house and build a new one in its place.

With four stories, a sandstone exterior, and a turret, the new home was a virtual castle. But it was the details within that truly made the home opulent. From the mosaic flooring to the doorknobs and hinges engraved with intricate scenes, nothing was overlooked in the design.

Hannes and Luise lived in the home for another 13 years, using the extra space to host German immigrants as they got on their feet. Sadly, heartache gripped the family once again in March of 1895 when Luise passed away in her bedroom.

A year later, Hannes sold the home. He would become the only surviving member of the family, losing his last child in 1906. The untimely deaths led to speculation that perhaps the family—or the home—was cursed.

For several decades, the place was used for various German clubs. By 1968, when the Romano family moved in, it already had a haunted reputation. The Romanos hoped to restore the home to its former glory. But as they polished away the tarnish of time, they uncovered more mysteries within the walls than they ever expected.

* * *

Early 1970s

Mrs. Romano had been determined to buy the home the moment she stepped inside. Despite her husband's protests, she would not be dissuaded. Something had drawn her to it.

Worn from years of community use, the place needed a lot of updates to restore its former glory. The Romanos settled in with their five children: two sets of twins just a year apart and a newborn baby.

The house was a web of mysteries, and the Romanos were intrigued by the secrets they found—including a Prohibition-era room hidden behind a panel. The chamber, likely sealed shut for decades, reeked of booze.

In their first months there, the Romanos started believing the rumors about ghosts. After playing in a room on the upper floor, the children often asked Mrs. Romano for a cookie to give the girl up there.

"She looks kind of funny in a really long dress and talks kind of funny too," her daughter told her. "She's so sad."

Mrs. Romano sprinkled the room with holy water, just in case it was more than an imaginary friend. But that was just the beginning of the haunted encounters. The girl in white, as she came to be known, became a regular specter in the home, as did a woman in black.

Between the sounds of chains being dragged across the floor, organ music (when there was no organ in the house), and objects disappearing, there were moments when Mrs. Romano thought she was losing her mind. In 1973, she even wrote to parapsychologist Hans Holzer, asking for help.

She sat at the bottom of the staircase. The house was getting to her again. It was almost like the air became thick, weighing her down with sorrow. But it wasn't her sorrow; it was Luise Tiedemann's—she was sure of it. Mrs. Romano's shoulders shook as she cried. There was so much loss and heartache, it was suffocating.

Luise was the strongest presence to Mrs. Romano—perhaps because Luise's spirit knew the woman could relate, since they were both mothers of large families. But there were many other spirits in the house. Although Mrs. Romano often felt overwhelmed by Luise's energy, she also felt protected by it. She needed that protection because the other spirits didn't seem nice.

At times, it felt as if the family was surrounded by spirits. On several nights, the Romanos heard babies wailing. Objects would be moved—not just across the room but from one floor to another.

Mrs. Romano seemed to take the brunt of it. She tried to make sense of what was happening, but when she spoke about it too much, she would become physically ill, as if the spirits were making her sick to keep her quiet.

Ghostly Tales of Ohio

One rumor that troubled her most was that a young girl was murdered on the fourth floor—hanged by her own father. Mrs. Romano couldn't find any proof of that, despite her best efforts.

She tried sitting for long periods of time at the Tiedemanns' gravesite, hoping they might reveal something to her. But if their souls knew the truth, they kept it buried with them.

Sitting on the steps, she could feel the spirits watching her. After pulling herself to her feet, she hurried out the back door. Her tension eased the moment she sat on the bench in the backyard. All the sorrow that sat heavily upon her seemed to catch in the breeze and blow away. Somehow, being out of the house made everything seem fine.

"It's not so bad," she said to herself, as if what she experienced in the home was perfectly normal.

She let the fresh air free her from the fear and sorrow. The children would be home from school soon. She should finish her work around the house before they arrived.

She took a deep breath and headed toward the door. "Everything is good," she told herself. She smiled at the imposing structure as she walked in its great shadow.

* * *

Her husband was working the night shift, and the children were asleep. Mrs. Romano debated having one of them stay in bed with her. She hated sleeping alone in this house. Still, despite it all, she loved the home in a way she couldn't explain.

To her relief, she fell asleep quickly. But she was awakened at midnight by the phone ringing.

"Hello?" Her voice was thick with sleep.

There was a pause, a breath on the other line. Then a voice unlike any she'd ever heard hissed, "Could I sleep with you tonight?"

Her mind crystalized with a flood of terror. She screamed, dropping the phone onto the floor. Her body shook uncontrollably as she remembered something Hans Holzer had told her: "Spirits can use phones to communicate."

The spirits wanted to frighten her, and she was utterly terrified. Yet she had no desire to leave this place. She felt possessed by it—like she and this place needed each other to survive.

* * *

The Romanos did sell the home in 1974. The new owner, Reverend Sam Muscatello, offered ghost tours of the place, an unconventional way to raise funds for reconfiguring the space as a church. The tours brought in enough cash to work toward his goal and to support a local food pantry.

The more time Sam spent in the house, the more convinced he became that it was truly haunted. He leaned into that belief and decided to make the tours even better. With several feet of space between the stone exterior and the inner brick walls—a design intended to aid in heating the home—there was plenty of space within the walls to move around. He was aware of other hidden passages in the home. Some were created for ease of movement by servants. Others seemed to hide spaces for more intriguing reasons, like the Prohibition-era room.

In 1975, Sam decided to install another secret passage. He created an opening in one of the walls and started to move through it. There, lying on the floor, covered in decades of dust, was a set of human bones.

The coroner determined that the bones had been there for an extremely long time, but he couldn't tell much else. "I don't know if the individual was 20 or 40 years old," the coroner said. "I can't tell if it was a man or a woman. Death occurred many years ago, but I doubt we'll ever know how long."

Another mystery was added to the Franklin Castle, fueling legends that would continue to grow.

* * *

The house changed hands several times over the years, until a homeless man set fire to it in 1999. His reason? He told police that he did it because the place was evil.

Today, the owners of the Franklin Castle dare guests to spend the night. Is the placed haunted by "evil" spirits? It's hard to say for certain, but legends have a way of transforming truth. The weight of rumors can bend history into a twisted mass of misinformation. Perhaps that's one reason the spirits won't rest in Franklin Castle. Of course, it's not the only reason. The seeds of truth can lie in even the darkest of tales. After all, the bones left crumbling between those walls didn't leave themselves there.

Ceely Rose House, Malabar Farm State Park
Lucas

Spring 1896

Twenty-three-year-old Celia "Ceely" Rose stood near the fence that separated her parents' property from the neighbors' farm. Her 16-year-old neighbor, Guy Berry, was plowing his family's cornfield.

Ceely was a young woman with developmental delays, which left her ostracized by her peers, who considered her strange and unsociable. She didn't have friends and kept to herself at home, where she lived with her parents, Rebecca and David Rose, and her older brother, 31-year-old Walter.

Like many young women, she dreamed about marriage and longed to have a family of her own. But she didn't know how to manage this longing for love.

She had a reputation as a bit of a nuisance to some of the single farmers. Her affections were ignored or even laughed at, so she turned her attention to Guy.

"Hello, Guy," Ceely called.

Guy nodded respectfully and replied in a kind way: "'Afternoon, Ceely."

"I've been so lonely these days," she said, adjusting a wreath of flowers she'd put on her head. "I don't have any friends to speak to or go walking with. The town socials are such a bore, I don't bother going anymore."

She smiled coyly as Guy glanced over his shoulder at her. He had just started to attend the socials and knew that Ceely was never asked to dance and didn't talk to the other girls.

She wasn't unattractive—with her blue eyes and round, rosy cheeks. She was just so odd. Her immature and inappropriate behavior put everyone off, so they avoided interacting with her. Guy felt bad for her. He understood that life was hard for Ceely, and he didn't want to add to that.

"You surprise me with how you've grown," she continued, settling herself on the fence and fiddling with a twig she'd broken off an overhead tree branch.

Guy wasn't sure how to respond. He knew she was flirting with him, but he wasn't interested. He also knew that his parents avoided the Rose family. Their gristmill was less than 20 yards from the Berrys' front porch, but the families had gone several years without so much as a "howdy" across the yard. There was quiet tension between them, so Ceely's affection would be frowned upon by both sides.

"Thanks," he replied. "I need to keep working."

He smiled politely and turned the plow in the other direction, hoping Ceely would be gone by the time he finished the next row, but she wasn't.

And so it began. Ceely seemed to know just where Guy would be as he did his daily chores, and she made sure to show up every day. She would ramble on for an hour or more, talking about nothing important, making it clear that she wanted Guy to court her.

Guy would never be interested. He tolerated her attention, never wanting to hurt her feelings. Even when she declared that they would marry in three years, he tried to be polite without letting her think he was in agreement.

This went on for weeks, despite Guy's best efforts to avoid her, until he'd finally had enough. He told his parents if she didn't leave him alone, he would run away.

His father approached Ceely's father and explained what was going on between the kids. Embarrassed, David Rose confronted Ceely and made it clear that she was to leave Guy alone. Her mother and brother also scolded Ceely for behaving in such a way.

By now, Ceely had convinced herself that she and Guy were destined to be together. In her mind, she believed that her family was keeping them apart—and she was determined to put an end to their interference.

* * *

June 24, 1896

Ceely moved about the kitchen, helping her mother get breakfast ready. She was rarely this helpful, so Rebecca appreciated her effort. Ceely took the pepper box and seasoned the cottage cheese for her family before setting it on the table.

Everyone helped themselves to the dish. Ceely watched as her father and brother took large helpings. She smiled as she sat with her family, watching them eat their breakfast heartily.

"Thank you for your help, Ceely," her mother said, spooning a bite of cottage cheese into her mouth.

"I'm happy to help," Ceely replied, moving the food around on her plate.

She pretended to eat the cottage cheese, but she didn't dare put any in her mouth. She knew something they didn't: The seasoning in the pepper box was rat poison. Soon she would be the only living member of the family.

They became gravely ill so quickly that poison was immediately suspected by the young doctor who tended to them. Unfortunately, there was little he could do. Ceely's father died first, followed by her brother.

Her mother had eaten much less than the men and, miraculously, was markedly better in less than two weeks. Rebecca was adamant that her daughter didn't do anything to hurt her family, that whatever had caused the terrible illness was a tragic accident.

As she regained her strength, Rebecca's appetite returned. She made herself a large bowl of cornbread and buttermilk. When she requested more, Ceely seized the opportunity and sprinkled the rat poison on it before bringing it to her. Shortly after finishing her meal, Rebecca began vomiting uncontrollably again.

As she struggled through another bout of agony, the reality of what was happening settled in. She told Ceely, "If it is you who's done this, God help you."

Not long after her mother's death, Ceely was arrested and charged with three counts of murder. The prosecution enlisted the help of Ceely's only childhood friend to help them get a confession.

Ceely told her old friend, "I could hardly keep from laughing as she was getting sick. The poison was working so well."

Ceely was found not guilty by reason of insanity. She lived the rest of her life in a psychiatric hospital and is buried in the hospital cemetery. Many believe that her spirit hasn't found rest.

* * *

Fall 2022

John listened intently as the tour guide stepped over the threshold into the kitchen of the Ceely Rose House. His 12-year-old granddaughter, Emma, stood beside him. The two shared a passion for history and were excited to find a time when the house, which was usually closed to visitors, offered a guided tour.

"This is the kitchen where Rebecca Rose spent a great deal of time preparing and preserving food for her family," the tour guide said. "It was reported that, when the family's belongings were auctioned off after their deaths, there was enough canned and preserved food to last a family one or two years."

"She was a hard worker," Emma said to her grandfather with a sad smile.

The history of the house was dark, but Emma had begged her grandfather to take her. He wondered, though, if it was too much.

The tour continued through the kitchen and into the living room. "David Rose survived for six days before succumbing to the poisoning in this room, lying on the couch. An autopsy was performed in the home, which revealed proof that he had been poisoned with arsenic."

The group followed the guide upstairs to the bedrooms. As they stood in one of them, Emma grabbed her grandfather's hand.

John looked down to see her staring at a rocking chair in the corner of the room. She had always been a psychically sensitive child, and John knew right away that she saw something he couldn't.

"What is it?" he asked quietly.

"I see Ceely sitting in that chair," Emma replied.

John squinted toward the chair and noticed that it rocked ever so slightly.

As the rest of the group moved into the hallway, the tour guide saw John and Emma watching the chair. Emma's face was white, and she was visibly shaken.

"Is everything okay?" the guide asked.

"This might sound crazy, but she's sensitive to spirits. She sees a woman in the chair."

"It doesn't sound crazy at all," the guide replied. "Years ago, a young boy was in this room talking to someone, but when his mother came in, she found that he was alone. When she asked who he was talking to, he explained that it was a woman in a white nightgown."

Emma looked at the guide, a sense of relief in her eyes. "You're not the only one who sees her," the guide said, patting her back.

People have been claiming to see Ceely for decades. There have been many reports of a woman, standing in the window, watching the area that used to be the fields where her beloved Guy worked. Her soul seems lost in longing for the love she would never share. Perhaps the irony isn't lost on her in the afterlife: In her plight to be loved, she killed the very people who loved her most.

Stetson House
Waynesville

December 1978

With Christmas right around the corner, the shops in Waynesville were bedazzled in decor. A layer of fresh snow gave the small community a nostalgic feel. The yellow home at 234 South Main Street, with its quaint front porch, could have been the image on a "Season's Greetings" postcard, with soft light emanating from the long front windows on both sides of the front door.

Built in the 1820s, the former home of Louisa Stetson Larrick now served as an antiques store. Marjorie Dodd, a retired teacher who now owned the place, delighted in calling this little piece of American history her own.

Louisa had lived in the home in the 1850s and 1860s. Between 1860 and 1865, her younger brother John Stetson stayed with her. He went on to design the first American cowboy hat, making the Stetson name iconic for decades to come.

Louisa's life had been less glamourous than her brother's, who would make millions. Married to a local farmer, who lived separately from her on the farm, her family struggled financially. She was reportedly unhappy, homesick, and bitter that her brother didn't help when he clearly had the means. After all, she had provided him with a home when he needed it, during difficult years.

Louisa passed away from consumption in the home in 1879, but it seems that her spirit never left.

Marjorie first heard about the place being haunted after a neighbor saw a woman, dressed in a Victorian gown, standing on the front porch at around 11 p.m. For a moment, the gentleman thought it odd that Marjorie would be at her shop so late—and odder yet that she was dressed in period clothing. It wasn't until the woman took a few steps and disappeared into the wall that he realized he was witnessing something paranormal.

Marjorie noticed some strange happenings as well. For instance, she'd leave the shop in pristine condition, only to find mirrors shattered on the floor when she returned. The nails on which they'd been hung were still firmly in the wall, the hanging wire perfectly intact. It made no sense, yet it happened far too often to be ignored.

Two older women entered the shop.

"Hello there," Marjorie called from the dining room, where she sat with her friend Dennis.

The women hustled over to her, their rosy cheeks raised with smiles.

"Mrs. Dodd?" one of them asked.

"That's right," Marjorie replied.

They excitedly introduced themselves as sisters who were former students. The three laughed, sharing memories of their time together in Marjorie's classroom. Soon, the pair wandered away to explore the treasures that Marjorie had cultivated within the old home.

It wasn't very long before they returned to the dining room.

"I can't believe this house could be haunted," one of the sisters said. "We've heard stories, but I don't believe there is anything to them."

The words had barely been spoken when a loud crash made them all jump. It was followed by a broken piece of glass in the shape of a chicken head, sliding across the floor and stopping inches from the women's feet.

They stared at the object with wide eyes, their mouths gaping.

Marjorie walked across the room and picked a glass dish off the floor; its lid had once been topped by the chicken head. She looked at the wall on the other side of the room, where the glass had been shelved.

"That didn't just fall off the shelf," Dennis observed. "It was thrown across the room."

"It sure was," Marjorie said. She smiled at her former students. "I guess the spirits here don't like to be doubted."

* * *

October 14, 1983

As a police cadet in Waynesville, it was Pat's job to help make sure the town stayed safe. He patrolled the streets at night, while residents slept peacefully in their homes. He didn't mind working the overnight shift. In fact, he enjoyed the quiet solitude, being alone with his thoughts.

On this night, he made his rounds on foot, as he usually did. It was around 3:45 a.m. A cool fall breeze rattled loose leaves on the trees. They dropped with a light clatter onto the pavement below. Pat made his way up the front steps of the Stetson House.

The antiques shop had recently been burglarized, so he wanted to make sure the place was secured. He jiggled the handle of the front door. Content that it was locked, he clopped down the steps and made his way to the sidewalk.

Before walking away, he glanced back. Something in the upstairs window caught his eye. The face of a man peered back at him.

His heart sank as he made eye contact with the man, who appeared to be around age 40. Pat was ready to call in another break-in, but before he could, the face began to fade. It felt like it happened in slow motion: The once-solid image became transparent. He could see through it yet still make out the features—particularly the man's prominent nose. And then the figure disappeared entirely.

It took a moment for Pat to steady himself. He knew the legends surrounding the house. He'd always chalked them up to people letting their imaginations get the better of them. But he couldn't deny what he'd just seen. Just as others had reported over the years, it seemed as if John Stetson had stopped by the old home that bore his name. Maybe he was paying his sister's spirit a visit, or maybe he was doing the same thing Pat was doing—making sure the old place was safe and secure.

Kelton House Museum
Columbus

Fernando Cortez Kelton was born in Vermont in 1812. A merchant, he moved to Ohio and became the first dry goods wholesaler in Columbus. In 1852, he and his wife, Sophia, built a house at 586 East Town Street for their family. At the time, their home was on the edge of town, bordered by pastureland.

Fernando and Sophia were passionate abolitionists and members of the town's anti-slavery society. Their home became a stop for escaping slaves on the Underground Railroad. The Kelton family even took in a sick 10-year-old escapee and raised her.

Fernando died in 1868, and Sophia remained in the family's home until her death in 1888. After her death, her son Ned (Edwin) and his wife, Laura, moved into the Kelton family home with their five daughters. Their youngest daughter, Grace, became the third-generation owner of the home. At her death in 1975, she gifted the home to the Columbus Foundation with the stipulation that it be preserved as a museum and used for educational purposes.

* * *

Summer 2018

Sally checked her watch. The guided tour would start in 10 minutes. Her friend Christine wrote ghost stories; anytime they traveled, Christine insisted that they find a historical tour—preferably one that was alleged to be haunted. As a history major herself, Sally never minded the tours, but she wasn't sure if she wanted to bump into an actual ghost.

Today's tour was of the Kelton House Museum and Garden.

Christine summarized some of the stories she'd read about the place. "Custodians have come to work to find their cleaning supplies all set out and ready for them."

"Interesting," said Sally.

They'd been best friends since high school and had been traveling together for nearly as long. Sally was used to her friend spouting off random facts about the places they visited, especially if those facts had anything to do with paranormal activities.

Christine continued, "Supposedly, Grace Kelton appears to visitors quite often and even joins in on tours."

"You don't really believe in that stuff, do you?" said a man, who was waiting with two friends for the tour to start.

Christine shrugged. "I guess we'll have to see if she shows up on our tour."

The man laughed. "The ghost stuff is fake. There's no way this place is haunted."

Unbeknownst to the man, their guide was listening patiently. "I hope, for your sake, that Grace doesn't hear you say that," she said.

"Oh yeah?" replied the man. "What would a ghost like Grace do to stop me?" His patronizing laughter grew louder.

The guide studied him for a minute and then started with her introduction. As the tour went on, the man grew increasingly rude, making fun of the guide and even the house itself.

With a sigh, the guide led the group upstairs. A smile grew across her face. "Sir, if you don't believe me, why don't you go spend some time in Grace's room?"

"What?" he asked.

"Grace's room. If you don't believe in ghosts and you think this is all a fraud, then there shouldn't be a problem, right?"

"That's ridiculous," said the man.

"Are you afraid?" asked his friend with a snicker.

"No!" the man answered too quickly.

The guide shrugged and continued showing everyone around.

When they had seen all of the rooms, the guide paused again at the top of the stairs. "Here's your last chance," she said to the man. "Or are you afraid of ghosts?"

"Of course, I'm not afraid," said the man, and he walked into the bedroom.

"What do you think is going to happen?" Sally asked Christine.

"Hopefully something spectacular," Christine said with a giggle.

As soon as she said the words, the man came out of Grace's room, pushed past the tour guide, and hurried down the stairs.

"What do you think happened?" Christine asked the tour guide.

The guide grinned. "Let's just say that Grace doesn't mess around. If she wants someone to know that she's here, she lets them know."

"Come on," said Sally, tugging Christine's arm. "We have to find out what happened."

They followed the man's friends out to the garden.

The man was pacing back and forth along the walk. "It was the craziest thing. This woman, she appeared out of nowhere." His teeth chattered, and he rubbed his arms. "She looked just like the old lady in the photos. And then, and then . . . ." His words trailed off and he was quiet.

"And then what?" asked his friend.

"She walked toward me."

"Do you think they faked it?" asked the other friend.

"Oh, no," said the man. "This was definitely real."

"How do you know?"

"Because she walked right through me, and I still can't warm up."

"I bet he's never going to make fun of any ghosts again," Sally whispered.

"I think you're absolutely right," Christine agreed.

Prospect Place
Trinway

In 1808, when George W. Adams was a child, his family moved to Ohio, where his father established a successful mill business. As a young man, George and his brother, Edward, owned a flour mill, a boat yard, and numerous warehouses. They also shipped goods like grain and flour via the canal, and George would often take the goods on flatboats himself.

Staunch abolitionists, George and his brother became active in the Underground Railroad. George became known as a conductor and would go himself or send trusted others to retrieve refugees, hiding them under the decks of his boats to bring them to safety.

George lost his first wife to illness in 1853. He remarried a much younger woman named Mary Jane Robinson and decided to build a mansion. George named his future home "Prospect Place" to invoke the prospect of a happy future. However, the night before they were scheduled to move in, it burned to the ground.

According to legend, a bricklayer on the work crew drunkenly admitted to arson, with the goal of securing more work for himself. In any event, the 29-room brick mansion was promptly rebuilt and completed in 1857.

From 1857 to 1865, it served as a station in the Underground Railroad. While slavery was illegal in Ohio, so was helping or harboring escaped slaves. One precautionary feature was a cistern in the cellar to provide an indoor water supply. This prevented slave catchers and bounty hunters from seeing how much water was being used.

* * *

Summer 1860

Dinner was finished, and it was growing dark outside. The obsessive pounding on the door grew louder and even more impatient. George sighed and came out of his study. Nothing good would come from someone pounding on the door at this time in the evening.

His wife, Mary Jane, stood in the foyer with the housekeeper, wringing her hands and looking worried.

George gently turned her toward the main stairs. "I've got this. Just go check on the children."

"But it's so late, and whoever it is sounds angry," said his wife.

"It will be okay." He kissed her on the forehead and nodded at the housekeeper. She nodded back and led Mrs. Adams up the stairs.

He waited until they were out of sight before opening the door.

An angry man stood on the front step. "I know you've got them here," he shouted.

"I don't know what you're talking about, Mr. . . . ." He let the words trail off.

"I know you've been hiding slaves. I've been watching you."

"I don't know what you are talking about," he said again, deciding that this man was either a bounty hunter or a slave catcher.

"It's illegal to harbor slaves," the man declared.

George looked past him to see that his ranch hand had come up from the barn and was leaning against a tree. He tipped his hat to George, and George gave him a nod.

"You best be going now," said George, shutting the door on the man.

He knew that everything was going to be taken care of, and there was nothing to worry about.

* * *

April 2013

Heather couldn't believe her luck. The old mansion was under renovation and usually only open for tours on weekends, but the owner had agreed to send a guide to meet her at the house and answer her questions for an article that she was writing.

She arrived a bit early, and rather than sit in her car, Heather decided to walk around the outside of the house, hoping it might inspire some additional questions. As she turned the corner of the house, near the barn, she suddenly regretted the idea. The barn felt ominous.

She retreated to her car. Her guide was just arriving.

"You must be Robert," she said. "Thank you so much for meeting me."

Ghostly Tales of Ohio

"We are all about preserving the history and telling the stories here," he replied. "I'm happy to share what I know. Is there anything special you want to see?"

"I've heard about the cistern in the basement," she said.

"Of course," he said, "but let's start in the barn and work our way inside."

Heather shivered from apprehension. She thought about disagreeing, but if there was something he wanted to show her, she should see it. Besides, maybe it wouldn't be as creepy with him leading the way. She followed him to the barn.

"The story in here," Robert explained, "isn't something we usually tell on the tours." He opened the door, letting in light to chase away the shadows.

"What happened in the barn?" she asked, already knowing that, whatever it was, it hadn't been good.

"One day, a bounty hunter came to the door, convinced that George Adams was part of the Underground Railroad. George sent him away, but George's employees were loyal to him. His ranch hand made sure that the man wouldn't spill the secret to anyone."

"What happened?" asked Heather, not sure she wanted to know.

"They hung him from the hayloft."

Chills danced down her back. A powerful blast of cold air rushed through the barn.

"I think he's probably still mad about it," she said.

"I'm sure he is," said Robert. "Our country was going through a tough time back then. The Civil War was amping up. There were choices to be made. I'm not one to say that the loss of a life was justified, but there is no doubt, if the story is true, it definitely preserved freedom for many others.

Heather felt the truth of the story in her bones. "Let's go see the house," she suggested.

Robert nodded. "Yes, it gets a little heavy out here." He led her back outside. "Up there." He pointed to the cupola on top of the house. "It's said that they would light a lantern to let others know it was safe to bring people here."

Robert led her into the house through the back door. Together, they toured the massive mansion. Robert pointed out various rooms of interest and talked about the painstaking process of restoring the building that, until recently, had been condemned and filled with graffiti. Heather could see the care that had gone into the home's restoration.

Finally, they went down to the basement.

"There's a story about a train crash, nearby," he explained. "It was a hot summer day in the late 1800s. Supposedly, this was the closest house, and there wasn't a hospital nearby. So they brought the injured here to the cool basement for medical help."

"Really?" Heather asked, scribbling a note. It wasn't about the Underground Railroad, but it was something interesting that she could try to confirm.

"As you might imagine, a lot of them died here."

She nodded.

A loud thump came from upstairs, adding an exclamation point to his statement.

Heather jumped, and Robert glanced up at the ceiling. Before he could comment, loud footsteps seemed to stomp across the floor above them.

Heather stared at Robert, not sure what question to ask.

A smile stretched across his face as he said, "Sometimes that happens."

She just looked at him, her eyes wide.

"Do you have any other questions?" he asked.

Heather wanted to ask if the place was haunted, but she was already sure she knew the answer. "No, I think we're good," she replied.

He led her upstairs. For comfort, Heather stayed right behind him.

Back outside, she was relieved to be in the fresh air. "If I come up with anything else, I know how to find you. Thank you again for your time."

She said goodbye to Robert and drove away from the intriguing and impressive property. As scared as she'd been in the moment, she was keenly aware that she'd been given a glimpse into something special. It was a house where the past reached into the present, reminding visitors not to forget.

Haunted Outdoor Spaces

Moonville Tunnel
McArthur

Deep in the heart of Zaleski State Forest, the hidden remnants of a long-gone railroad community lie beneath the overgrowth of bushes. Lost to time, Moonville was hardly a town, even at its peak. It was a sparse collection of homes for miners and railroad workers, spread out within walking distance of the local train station.

Little can be found of the former community, except for the foundation of the schoolhouse, the community cemetery, and the old train tunnel built through a hill. Long and narrow, the tunnel provided trains with a route through the hillside for more than 100 years, until the railroad line was abandoned in the mid-1980s.

During its years of operation, this stretch of railroad was the site of more than one death. From people being struck as they walked through the tunnel to a landslide striking a locomotive as it barreled down the tracks, historical documents indicate that more than 20 people lost their lives there.

With so many sudden deaths in one place, it's no surprise that ghosts lurk in the shadows of the abandoned tunnel.

* * *

January 1895

William Washburn kept his eyes focused ahead as the engine he oversaw shuttled over the tracks, bound for Moonville. He was only about a half mile away and was due to arrive at Moonville Station at 8:50 p.m.

"We've made good time," Conductor Charles Bazler said, stepping into the cab behind him.

"A speedy, uneventful trip, just how I like them," William replied.

He enjoyed trips with Charles, who kept the crew in line with his calm-yet-firm demeanor. Charles respected the crew, and in turn, they respected him. It made William's job easier, knowing that things were running smoothly in the cars he pulled behind him.

"Do you see that?" Charles asked, his tone suddenly tense.

William saw it: the ghost of Moonville.

The figure of a man stood in the center of the track. A white cape billowed in the breeze as the ghostly spectral with a long white beard waved a lantern in front of him. No one had seen the ghost in a year now, but it had often been reported at this exact location in previous years—after a deadly collision between two freight trains took place five years earlier.

William didn't respond to Charles. Shock seemed to trap the words in his throat, beneath a lump of fear that he thought might suffocate him. He reached out and blew the whistle, more out of reflex than conscious effort.

The being seemed to stare through William. Its eyes glowed like balls of fire. Unflinching, the figure—with an unearthly halo of light emanating from it—continued to swing the lantern as if desperate to warn William of danger.

William blasted the whistle again, as the train closed in on the apparition. Just before being struck by the locomotive, the spectral moved off the track, disappearing into the nearby rocks.

Many believe the ghost to be that of Engineer Lawhead, who lost his life in a crash. Was the doomed man stuck in an eternal loop, desperately trying to warn other engineers of an impending disaster that he couldn't understand had already passed?

Although this was the first ghost reported along those tracks, it wouldn't be the last.

* * *

The ghost of David Keeton, a man around the age of 66, is said to haunt the tracks around Moonville Tunnel. His spirit reportedly pesters people by throwing stones at them.

David's mangled body was found near the tunnel after being run over by multiple trains throughout the early hours of Sunday, June 27, 1886. News accounts stated that parts of him were never recovered.

According to some reports, he likely stopped to rest on the tracks. After falling asleep, he was hit by the very train he'd been hoping to catch to take him home. Other rumors suggest that he was murdered. Some lore casts David as a local bully called "Baldie," who was known to pick fights and torment those he considered weak. Of course, legends have a way of making monsters out of mortals, even if there isn't evidence to support such a dark legacy. What is known for sure about David is that he was passing through Moonville due to a lawsuit, and when he died, he left behind a wife and six grown children.

* * *

Another ghost around the tunnel is that of an older woman. She was hit by a train while collecting lavender. People report seeing her spirit in period clothing. The sightings are often accompanied by the scent of lavender, which is how this spectral came to be known as the Lavender Lady.

Today, the abandoned railroad line serves as walking and biking trails for visitors of the Zaleski State Forest. Its haunted history is openly celebrated with the annual "Midnight at Moonville" festival each October.

The Collinwood School Fire
Collinwood

Lake View School was built in Collinwood in 1902, with the dedicated purpose of educating the ever-growing immigrant population, teaching the children about the economic and political systems of the country. Within four years, the school needed to double its size.

The impressive and imposing three-story building promised to shape young hearts and minds. However, forward-thinking architects in other parts of the country were already building schools with sealed stairways and noncombustible materials. None of that was a concern at the Lake View School, but it should have been.

* * *

Ash Wednesday, March 4, 1908

Fritz Hirter, the custodian of Lake View School, arrived to stoke the school's furnace in the early morning hours. By 6:30 a.m., he was cleaning classrooms and sweeping the hallways, getting ready for the day. At 8 a.m., he unlocked the doors for the school's 366 enrolled students, including four of his own children.

With the students in their classrooms, Fritz went into the basement to sweep. It wasn't long before he caught a whiff of smoke. His eyes saw what his nose had already determined: Smoke was wafting out from under the stairs. He ran to the fire alarm to alert the students and teachers.

Unbeknownst to anyone, at some point during those morning hours, the steam pipes running under the first floor of the school began to overheat. Touching upon the wooden joists, the boiling-hot pipes caused a flame to burst forth.

Fritz ran to open the doors, first the front and then the back. However, the air that came rushing through the building served to fan the flames, so the doors were closed again. Rushing to the classrooms, he yelled for the children to leave. Finding his 5-year-old daughter, Ida, he rushed her out the door.

The building was quickly engulfed in flames, and chaos reigned. As children tripped and fell, the rush of panicked classmates trying to escape became a pile of fear. Fritz spotted his daughter Helena among them and tried to reach her, but a wall of fire pushed him back.

Ten-year-old Hugh, son of the chief of police, led several children to the fire escape. When a few saw that they would have to jump down to the grass, they ran back into the building. Hugh rushed after them to try and save them; he was never seen again.

Narrow stairways, packed with children and blocked by flames, left many students with nowhere to go. With

110 *Ghostly Tales of Ohio*

more and more children trying to escape from the second and third floors, many of them wedged together against the front and rear doors, which they couldn't open.

Townspeople ran from everywhere to try and help. When they finally got the front door open, rescuers were horrified to find piles of children who had been trampled and burned. One such rescuer, Wallace Upton, spotted his 10-year-old daughter, still alive, underneath several dead children. He struggled to try and free her, suffering horrible burns in the process. But as the flames closed in, he was unable to pull her to safety.

Inside, Fritz was able to save several children by pulling them out of the tangled mess and tossing them out a window. He worked until his hands were burned, only saving himself as the floor began to crumble beneath him.

Within an hour, the fire mostly burned itself out. Mercifully, the fragile walls remained intact for what became a recovery mission. In all, 172 children, 2 teachers, and 1 rescuer had perished. Some bodies were never recovered, believed to have been reduced to ashes in the rubble.

Throughout the town, white ribbons were placed on the front doors of homes where a child had been lost. Several bodies that could not be identified were buried together in a mass grave at the Lake View Cemetery. Children from poor families were given a white coffin and included in this plot.

The town needed a new school. While several families were opposed, the decision was made to build the new one next to the place where the old one once stood. The new school, Collinwood Memorial, opened in 1910.

* * *
Cleveland, June 1999

Christina's roommate and good friend, Christopher, let the door to their house slam shut behind him.

He excitedly told her, "I just borrowed a documentary about the Collinwood school fire. Do you want to watch it?"

"The Collinwood school fire?" asked Christina.

"Yeah, in 1908. It was the deadliest fire in American history." He put the movie into the VCR and turned on the television.

For the next hour, they were engrossed in the horror of the tragic fire. When the documentary ended, they sat together, processing the depths of the story they'd just watched.

"Want to go see where it happened?" he asked. He pulled a map off the shelf. "I think it's only 15 minutes from here." He flipped open the map and pointed to the streets.

Christina nodded. "Okay, let's go."

It didn't take them long to find the school. The roommates parked and walked together to the large memorial.

"This is the exact spot where the old school once stood," read Christina.

The hair on her arms stood at attention as shivers raced down her back. The fiery images from the documentary were still fresh in her mind. Being at the actual site of the tragedy was surreal.

Christina moved slowly around the square, reading every name. Their photos, shown at the end of the documentary, flashed into her mind.

When she finished, she took a deep breath to hold back the tears and looked around the park. There was litter everywhere.

She started picking up the garbage, happy for a distraction. As she worked, Christina became overwhelmed with sadness, beyond what she had felt moments ago. This sadness was different—bigger. It was like she'd walked into a bubble of sadness that she knew wasn't her own.

Suddenly, Christina felt a child's hand slip into hers. Surprised, she froze. Her heart felt like it was going to beat out of her chest. The phantom hand touched her back, then slowly moved down the back of her leg. It felt like a small child, trying to cling to its mother.

As startling as it was, the invisible touch was somehow comforting. Standing in the park she's just tidied, picking up garbage that wasn't hers, holding the hand of a child's spirit, Christina was able to offer a small act of kindness to honor those who lost their lives on that horrific day.

* * *

By the 1970s, the Collinwood Memorial School was abandoned. It remained vacant for decades. There were many reports of neighbors hearing children cry out from within its walls. Sometimes, little faces could be seen, peering out from the windows late at night. Cold spots and creepy corners (unsettling places) were reported by those who ventured inside after dark. An inexplicable light was often seen, moving about the second floor. Sometimes, the park itself would smell so heavily of smoke that it kept visitors at bay.

Ghostly Tales of Ohio

The long-vacant school was finally demolished in 2004, and a new school has been built in its place. Nevertheless, the massive tragedy and the terror of that day surely imprinted on the space. The sadness and grief of parents who lost their children would hang heavy in the air for decades to come. Perhaps now, enough time has passed that the souls have finally settled.

Frankenstein's Castle
Kettering

May 17, 1967

It was as if the sky had been ripped open and water was being dumped from buckets by an angry god. The rain came down in sheets, with great gusts of wind blowing the branches wildly above the two teens, running toward the imposing stone tower.

They hadn't been expecting rain. If they had, they wouldn't have gone driving in Ronnie's convertible. Sixteen-year-old Peggy had recently gotten her driver's permit, and Ronnie was happy to give her lessons. A year older than Peggy, Ronnie loved spending time with her. She was cute and fun to be around—the kind of girl that everyone liked. He was lucky to be her boyfriend.

The two had rushed from the car toward the tower, hoping to wait out the rain someplace dry. But when they pushed through the gated door, they found that the tower had no roof.

Set atop a hill, the tower had been constructed with salvaged stones from buildings that were condemned by the city. The first stones were laid in 1940, and the tower was completed the following year. With 3-foot-thick walls and a winding staircase that led to the top of the 56-foot structure, it was intended as a place for locals to enjoy the view of the park and golf course below.

Sadly, it instead became a place where teens came to drink and cause trouble—some even throwing beer bottles at vehicles below. The city blocked the door with a locked iron gate, hoping to deter the behavior. But teens kept finding ways to unlock it.

Ronnie and Peggy hadn't come to the tower for trouble. They simply wanted to get out of the rain.

It was around 7 p.m., when the sky lit up with a massive flash. The tower, the tallest point around, was a natural attraction for the lightning bolt that ripped through the dark clouds.

It's unclear whether the couple was walking up the steps or coming down them. Some speculated that Peggy was touching the drenched stone wall with the right side of her body, perhaps leaning on it. Others suggested that a fireball may have been produced by the strike and that Peggy took the brunt of the flames. Regardless of how, she suffered first-, second-, and third-degree burns over most of the right half of her body.

Ronnie was in a daze when he was found, lying on the ground, halfway outside the door. Ronnie survived his injuries. Tragically, Peggy was found dead about 10 steps up the staircase.

The doorway was sealed with concrete, but legends claim that the step where Peggy died still bears the burn marks left behind. If the other rumors are true, that's not the only haunting reminder of the tragedy.

* * *

Fall 1995

Scott parked his car and looked up at the imposing brick structure in front of them. He turned off his headlights, leaving the wooded area in shadowy darkness. The gray stone structure was lit by the moon, which dipped behind clouds as a storm blew in.

"It looks like a castle," Allison said in awe.

"I suppose that's why they call it Frankenstein's Castle," Scott replied.

"Some people call it Witch's Tower or Petterson's Castle," Allision said. "I think when they built it, they just called it Lookout Tower."

"Whatever they call it, it's creepy," Melissa said with a shiver.

"That's why we're here: because it's haunted, right?" Brad added.

"I guess," Melissa replied. "But this wasn't my idea. I'm just here as emotional support for the three of you when you get totally freaked out."

The couples got out of the car, each with a flashlight in their hands, and made their way up the hill. They stopped in front of the door, sealed shut with concrete. They walked around the sandy path encircling the tower. Beyond it were dense trees, giving the tower an eerie sense of seclusion from the world.

"Why do they really call it Frankenstein's Castle?" Melissa asked.

"Maybe because of the lightning strike," Brad suggested. "Do you remember that scene in the movie

Ghostly Tales of Ohio

when Frankenstein's monster comes alive after the lighting strikes?"

"I guess that sort of makes sense," Melissa said, shining her flashlight around.

It was sad to realize that, in this case, lightning had the opposite effect—and it wasn't a monster whose life was impacted by the electrical bolt. It was a girl about her age.

In the distance, a flash lit up a dark cloud. An accompanying rumble followed several seconds later.

"It's not too close yet," Scott said.

Everyone seemed to be holding their breath, listening for any sounds that would fit the legend. Supposedly, on stormy nights, people heard crying and moaning coming from the tower. Some even reported seeing a girl and a boy.

There were no cries for help or quiet sobs now, though. It was utterly quiet.

"Apparently, they had to handcuff Ronnie to get him in the ambulance. He was hysterical," Allison said, sharing what she'd learned while researching the place.

"I would have been losing my mind, too, if I just saw my girlfriend get killed," Scott said.

The four exchanged sad glances, the gravity of what had happened sinking in. Their moment of silence was interrupted by another burst of light. This time, the clap of thunder came more quickly.

"I still don't think it's too close," Scott said. "But we'd better get back in the car to be safe."

The four started down the hill. They were almost to the bottom when they heard it: Soft and barely audible, somewhere in the distance was the sound of a muffled whimper.

They all froze.

"Maybe it's a cat?" Brad reasoned.

They turned and looked back toward the tower, just as another shock of light lit up the sky. Melissa gasped as she saw what appeared to be the shadowy figure of a girl, silhouetted against the white concrete of the sealed door.

The boom that accompanied the lightning made Melissa's head rattle. She closed her eyes against the deafening sound. When she opened them, the figure was gone.

The thunder seemed to crack open the clouds, and a torrent of rain came rushing down—massive drops pelting their skin as they sprinted to the car.

As Scott drove away from the park, Melissa thought she must have imagined the shadow of the girl.

But then Brad asked, "Did anyone else see her?"

Allison turned to face the backseat, looking from Brad to Melissa. Her eyes were wide, her expression solemn. "Yes," she nodded.

Melissa nodded back. "Me too."

Scott kept his eyes on the road, the wipers moving furiously across the windshield. "Yeah," he added.

Perhaps the haunting at Frankenstein's Tower is like a suppressed memory. When Mother Nature brings in a storm, the tragedy that scarred the tower flickers to the surface of consciousness for just a moment before getting pushed down again—until the next storm rolls in, and the memory rises again.

Spring House Gazebo in Eden Park
Cincinnati

October 6, 1927

Imogene Remus smoothed out the skirt of her black dress, took a deep breath, and rested her head on the back of the taxi seat as they drove through Walnut Hills. Black seemed an appropriate color for the day. She was on her way to her attorney's office to prepare for the divorce hearing later that afternoon. Her 19-year-old daughter, Ruth, sat beside her.

Imogene never could have imagined the recent turns her life would take. When she met her second husband, George Remus, she had been a young mother, pursuing a divorce from her first husband. George was a well-respected lawyer, known for handling high-profile criminal cases. He was also married.

George had quickly become smitten with the dark-haired beauty and her vivacious personality. He wasn't shy about letting her know. He bought her expensive things and soon hired her as his secretary. It wasn't long before both Imogene and George were legally disentangled from their spouses and free to marry each other, which they did in 1920.

Now, seven years later, they were headed toward the bitter end of their once-fiery romance. In that time, George traded practicing law in Chicago for dealing in illegal alcohol in Cincinnati. Soon he was known as the "king of bootleggers."

After her husband's arrest and imprisonment in 1924, Imogene found herself embroiled in a love affair with Franklin Dodge, a Federal Bureau of Investigation agent who had played a key role in her husband's arrest.

When George found out, he was livid. Imogene feared that she might not be safe. Her husband was a well-connected and dangerous man. She had no idea that her husband was in another vehicle, following her—or that he had been lying in wait at a nearby hotel since being released from prison three days earlier, waiting for the right moment to attack.

* * *

"Pull over in front of them," George instructed his chauffeur.

Without hesitation, the man did as he was told. You didn't ignore the demands of George Remus if you knew what was good for you.

Imogene's taxi driver swerved into the curb to avoid hitting the vehicle, lurching Imogene forward in her seat. When she looked out at the car that had cut them off, her heart sank.

"Go!" she screamed at the driver.

Ghostly Tales of Ohio **121**

Ruth, eyes wide with fear, held her breath as the taxi accelerated. The car swerved in front of them again, this time causing the taxi to slam to a stop.

Imogene was out the door before the driver could process what was happening. She ran into Eden Park, screaming.

Within seconds, George caught up with her, grabbed her by the wrist, and pulled her to him. In the shadow of the Spring House Gazebo, Imogene was face to face with the man she once loved, the barrel of his revolver pressed into her abdomen.

"Please, don't," she cried.

For a brief second, she thought she saw a glimmer of the passion she'd seen as they were falling in love. But love and hate could burn simultaneously, and passion could shift to loathing with the single beat of a heart.

A gunshot rang out. George released his wife from his arms, and she dropped to the ground, holding her stomach.

Imogene was rushed to a hospital, where she died 2 hours later.

Three months after murdering his wife in broad daylight, George Remus was found not guilty by reason of insanity, claiming that his wife's affair with Franklin Dodge—along with their alleged conspiracy to liquidate his assets, take his money, and put out a hit on him—had driven him mad.

After his trial, George had a brief stay at a psychiatric hospital before being released. While George moved on, it seems Imogene did not. Denied justice, her spirit has restlessly wandered the park where she was murdered in cold blood.

* * *

August 2024

A light breeze rustled the leaves as Stacy made her way along the paths in Eden Park. This was her favorite place to unwind after a long day. Breathing in the fresh air, surrounded by nature, she could almost forget that she was in the heart of a big city. She loved all that Cincinnati had to offer, but the tranquility of the park gave her a sense of stillness that helped her stay grounded.

The sun was beginning to dip lower in the sky, but she still had plenty of daylight left. The sound of the fountain, raining into the lake beside her, paired with the birds chirping to create a beautiful melody. Stacy smiled, taking it all in.

As she rounded the edge of the lake near the Spring House Gazebo, she noticed movement in the shadows between the structure and the walking path. A woman moved solemnly. Dressed in a black dress and wearing a black hat, she looked as if she'd stepped out of a 1920s-era film.

Despite the August heat, Stacy's arms prickled with goosebumps. Instinctively, she knew that she was seeing something otherworldly. She'd heard the legend of Imogene Remus's ghost haunting the park. Some described her as a woman in white. Others reported her exactly as Stacy was seeing her: dressed in black, as she had been on the day she died.

Stacy watched in disbelief. The woman looked at her, longingly. Stacy had the strange sense that the woman was looking through her, that she didn't notice Stacy at all.

Slowly, the woman began walking toward the lake. Like an old roll of film breaking away from a reel, the woman flickered and then disappeared completely.

The encounter was only seconds long, but Stacy had no doubt about what she'd seen. The restless, troubled soul of Imogene Remus had shown herself.

Perhaps she is still searching for justice, trapped in the sorrow and regret of a life embroiled in scandal, wishing for the opportunity to choose differently.

Bibliography

PREFACE

History.com Editors. "Ohio." History (history.com). Accessed on March 31, 2025.

No author. "Ohio Reformatory's Haunted History." Travel Channel (travelchannel.com). Accessed on October 20, 2024.

OHIO STATE REFORMATORY *(Mansfield)*

Bagans, Zak and Nick Groff. Written by Belanger, Jeff, Nick Groff, and Zak Bagans. "Ohio Reformatory." *Ghost Adventures* (Season 3, Episode 3). November 20, 2009.

Kish, Elaine. "Ohio State Reformatory." Compass Ohio (compassohio.com). Accessed on October 27, 2024.

No author. "Haunted Places Series: Ohio State Reformatory." National Property Inspections (npiweb.com). October 3, 2022.

No author. "Ohio Reformatory's Haunted History." Travel Channel (travelchannel.com). Accessed on October 20, 2024.

No author. "About the Ohio State Reformatory." The Ohio State Reformatory (mrps.org). Accessed on October 20, 2024.

Staff Writer. "Inmate Burns Self to Death at OSR." *News Journal*. February 6, 1960.

GORE ORPHANAGE *(Amherst)*

Dray, April. "The Most Terrifying Ghost Story To Ever Come Out of Ohio is Truly Terrifying." Only in Your State (onlyinyourstate.com). December 24, 2022.

No author. "The Haunting History of Gore Orphanage & Swifts Hollow." Vermilion Chamber of Commerce (vermillionohio.com). Accessed on November 7, 2024.

Tarrant, Rich. "Gore Orphanage: The Real Story." (vermilionohio.com). July 1, 2003.

THE COLLINGWOOD ART CENTER *(Toledo)*
Carr, Julie. "Toledo, Ohio: Collingwood Art Center." HauntedHouses.com (hauntedhouses.com). Accessed on March 30, 2025.

Cheaib, Zeinab. "Is the Collingwood Arts Center the most haunted building in Toledo?" WTOL11 (wtol.com).

Johnson, Scott A. "Cold Spots: The Collingwood Arts Center." Dread Center (dreadcentral.com). May 15, 2009.

SEDAMSVILLE RECTORY *(Cincinnati)*
No author. "Sedamsville Rectory." Cincinnati Ghosts (cincinnatighosts.com). May 7, 2024. Updated November 21, 2024.

Rasmussen, Ragnarr. "The Haunted History of Sedamsville Rectory: A Hotspot for Paranormal Activity." Medium (medium.com). November 23, 2024.

Rick. "The Sedamsville Rectory." Creepy Cincinnati: Cincinnati Hauntings & Urban Legends. July 16, 2016.

LAKE ERIE COLLEGE *(Painsville)*
Farkas, Karen. "Myths and legends on college campuses still resonate." Cleveland.com (cleveland.com). January 12, 2013.

No Author. "History of Lake Erie College." Lake Erie College (lec.edu). Accessed on March 29, 2025.

Young, Jay. "Ohio College Ghost Stories: The Legend of Tiberius." College Bound Advantage (collegeboundadvantage.com). October 3, 2019.

LICKING COUNTY HISTORIC JAIL *(Newark)*
Belanger, Jeff. "Old Licking County Jail." *Ghost Adventures* (Season 9, Episode 13). Aired July 12, 2014.

Goth, Mitch. "Old Licking County Jail." Haunted US (hauntedus.com). Accessed on March 30, 2025.

Muhammad, Mariyam. "24 haunted places in Ohio you should visit." The Cincinnati Enquirer. October 12, 2024.

No author. "Carl Mayes Etherington." Find a Grave (findagrave.com). Accessed on March 30, 2025.

No author. "Deputy Marshal Carl Mayes Etherington." Officer Down Memorial Page (odmp.org). Accessed on March 30, 2025.

No author. "Harwell Etherington." Find a Grave (findagrave.com). Accessed on March 30, 2025.

Smith, Darrin. Personal Interview conducted by Jessica Freeburg on March 31, 2025.

Staff Writer. "Jailed Woman Dies of Burns." *The Sandusky Register.* July 15, 2953.

THE MOLLY STARK SANATORIUM *(Louisville)*

Balint, Ed. "Molly Stark haunted? Visitors to former tuberculosis clinic say they have witnessed strange, unexplainable happenings." Canton Rep: The Repository (cantonrep.com). October 24, 2015.

Curious History. "Molly Stark Sanatorium: A True Horror Story." YouTube (youtube.com). October 25, 2021.

No author. "The Haunted Molly Stark Hospital." Haunted Rooms America (hauntedrooms.com). Accessed on January 30, 2025.

No author. "Molly Stark Sanatorium." U.S. Ghost Adventures. (usghostadventures.com). October 22, 2022.

THE WILLOUGHBY MEDICAL CENTER *(Willoughby)*

No Author. "Old Print Article: Confessions of A Body Snatcher, New York Times (1878)." Afflictor (afflictor.com). October 3, 2013.

Norman, Michael. "Haunted Ohio: 'America's Most Haunted' puts the spotlight on Willoughby…" Cleveland.com (cleveland.com). September 24, 2014.

Taddeo MD, Ronald J., "Willoughby, Ohio: Our History." Willoughby, Ohio (willoughbyohio.com). Accessed on March 26, 2025.

THE RIDGES *(Athens)*

H., Jim. "Decomposed Body Stain of Margaret Shilling." Historic Mysteries (historicmysteries.com). December 5, 2015.

Johnson, Alan. "Revolution in Mental Health Care: The Athens Lunatic Asylum." Ohio History Connection (ohiohistory.org). January/February 2024.

No author. "History of the Ridges." Ohio University (ohio.edu). Accessed on March 2, 2025.

Staff Writer. "Woman, 53, Found Dead." *The Times Recorder*. January 13, 1979.

Young, Jay. "Ohio College Ghost Stories: The Legend of the Ridges." College Bound Advantage (collegeboundadvantage.com). October 30, 2019.

Zimmermann, Carolyn M., Unige A. Laskay, and Glen P. Jackson. "Analysis of Suspected Trace Human Remains from an Indoor Concrete Surface." *J Forensic Sci.* (Vol. 53, No. 6). November 2008.

BUXTON INN *(Granville)*

Jones, Jennifer. "The Haunted Buxton Inn's Ghostly Guests." The Dead History (thedeadhistory.com). May 22, 2022.

No Author. "About." Buxton Inn (buxtoninn.com). Accessed on March 15, 2025.

WOSU Public Media. "Ghosts, History, and the Underground Railroad: Granville Ohio's Buxton Inn." YouTube (youtube.com). October 29, 2024.

THE LAYFAYETTE HOTEL *(Marietta)*

No author. "The Lafayette: A Grand Riverboat Era Hotel—Our History." Lafayette Hotel (lafayettehotel.com). Accessed on March 16, 2025.

Sellman, Lindsey. "Haunted Ohio: The Lafayette Hotel." *Ohio Magazine* (ohiomagazine.com). September/October 2020.

Williams, Mark. "LaFayette Hotel has storied past." *The Ironton Tribune* (irontontribune.com). October 29, 2021.

PARK HOTEL *(Put-in-Bay)*
Copenhaven, Beth. "The Historic Park Hotel in Ohio is Notoriously Haunted and We Dare You to Spend the Night." Only In Your State (onlyinyourstate.com). August 13, 2021.

No Author. "10 Haunted Ohio Hotels: The Most Haunted Places in Ohio." Heritage Ohio (heritageohio.org) Accessed on March 29, 2025.

No Author. "Put-in-Bay Hotel History." Put-in-Bay Hotels (putinbayhotels.com). January 17, 2023.

Supernatural Occurrence Studies Podcast. "Live from HAUNTED Park Hotel—Put-in-Bay, OH." YouTube (youtube.com). September 16, 2018.

PUNDERSON MANOR *(Newberry Township)*
Chojnacki, Linda. "Punderson's Haunted History Tour showcases the lode's mystical past." *The Plain Dealer*. December 28, 2012.

King, Dominique. "Punderson's Haunted History." State of Ohio (ohio.org). October 5, 2022.

No Author. "10 Haunted Ohio Hotels: The Most Haunted Places in Ohio." Heritage Ohio (heritageohio.org). Accessed on March 30, 2025.

Staff Writer. "That Big House." *The Cleveland Press*. June 13, 1934.

THE GOLDEN LAMB *(Lebanon)*
No Author. "Historical Site: The Golden Lamb Inn." Daughters of the American Revolution (dar.org). Accessed on April 2, 2025.

No Author. "Lebanon: History of the City." Lebanon, Ohio (lebanonohio.gov). Accessed on April 2, 2025.

No Author. "The Most Haunted Hotels In Cincinnati." Cincinnati Ghosts (cincinnatighosts.com). February 28, 2025.

THE AKRON CIVIC THEATER *(Akron)*
Angela. "Ghostly Janitor Rescues Damsel in Distress at the Akron Theater." BoiC.G.H. (boiseghost.org). December 9, 2021.

Carr, Julie. "Akron, Ohio: The Akron Civic Theater." HauntedHouses.com (hauntedhouses.com). Accessed on March 22, 2025.

Conn, Jennifer. "Renovated, expanded Akron Civic Theater adds 2 stages: deck and video wall overlook Lock 3." Spectrum News 1 (spectrumnews1.com). April 17, 2021.

Kleen, M.A. "Mysterious America: Akron Civic Theater's Ghostly Trio." M.A. Kleen (michaelkleen.com). October 4, 2017.

Unknown Author. "Amish Country in Ohio." *Nan Miller Times* (nanmillertimes.com). April 30, 2018.

Weirdness Really Bad Movie. "Ghosts of The Akron Civic Theater." YouTube (youtube.com). September 24, 2011.

FRANKLIN CASTLE *(Cleveland)*

Feldhausen, Sandy. "The Mystery of Franklin Castle." *The Cleveland Press*. July 31, 1971.

Kaib, Tom. "A Tale for Halloween: Spooks Abound in Westside Castle." *The Plain Dealer*. October 28, 1973.

Kay, Leslie. "Old castle's present, past riddled with fiction, fact." *The Plain Dealer*. May 11, 1975.

Staff Writer. "Human Bones Found in 'Haunted' House." *St. Joseph News-Press*. January 19, 1975.

WKYC Channel 3. "Peek inside Ohio City's 'haunted' Franklin Castle." YouTube (youtube.com). October 30, 2019.

CEELY ROSE HOUSE, MALABAR FARM STATE PARK *(Lucas)*

No Author. "Ceely Rose House." Ohio Department of Natural Resources (ohiodnr.gov). Accessed on March 9, 2025.

Staff Writer. "Celia Rose Acquitted." *The Union County Journal*. October 22, 1896.

Staff Writer. "Celia Rose Awaits Trial for Murdering Three Persons." *Chicago Tribune*. August 17, 1896.

Staff Writer. "Celia Rose Indicted." *Maretta Daily Leader.* September 22, 1896.

Staff Writer "Her Terrible Revenge, Celia Rose Put Poison in the Family's Food." *The Leader Enterprise.* August 20, 1896.

Staff Writer. "On Trial for Murder." *The Cleveland Leader.* October 15, 1896.

STETSON HOUSE *(Waynesville)*
Callahan, Beth. "Stetson Hats and An 1879 Triple Hatchet Murder Just a Small Part of Waynesville's Past." *The Warren County Post* (warrencountypost.com). August 9, 2022.

Couch, Erin. "3 spooky sites in Ohio's 'most haunted town.'" *The Cincinnati Enquirer.* October 31, 2023.

Couch, Erin. "Ohio's 'most haunted town' is home to 3 spine-chilling sites. Read if you dare." *The Cincinnati Enquirer.* October 25, 2023.

McKnight, Joe B. "Stetson house throws hat in to the realm of the haunted." *News Journal.* October 30, 1983.

THE KELTON HOUSE MUSEUM *(Columbus)*
Angela. "Never Poke Fun At The Paranormal: The Kelton House Museum And Garden." BoiC.G.H. (boiseghost.org). May 28, 2022.

Fuller, Yates. "Martha Hartway (1858-1924)." Black Past (blackpast.org). April 26, 2020.

No Author. "Fernando Cortez Kelton." Find A Grave (findagrave.com). Accessed on April 5, 2025.

No Author. "Haunted Columbus: Ghost stories from Kelton House Museum." 614 Now (614now.com). September 28, 2022.

No Author. Kelton House Museum & Garden. (keltonhouse.com). Accessed on April 5, 2025.

No Author. "Underground Railroad: Kelton House." Teaching Columbus Historic Places. (teachingcolumbus.omeka.net). Accessed on April 5, 2025.

PROSPECT PLACE *(Trinway)*

Oborn, Alison. "Prospect Place Ghosts, Ohio." Adelaide's Haunted Horizons (adelaidehauntedhorizons.com.au). Accessed on April 6, 2025.

No Author. "Prospect Place." Haunted U.S. (hauntedus.com). Accessed on April 6, 2025.

No Author. "Prospect Place: The Ohio House That Is Haunted By History." American Hauntings (americanhauntingsink.com). Accessed on April 6, 2025.

No Author. "Historic Prospect Place Estate: Home of the G.W. Adams Educational Center." G.W. Adams Educational Center (gwacenter.org). Accessed on April 6, 2025.

MOONVILLE TUNNEL *(McArthur)*

Gottsacker, Erin. "How the ghosts of Moonville are keeping the town's history alive." Statehouse News Bureau (statenews.org). October 12, 2023.

No Author. "Moonville Tunnel." Ohio Department of Natural Resources (ohiodnr.gov). Accessed on March 9, 2025.

Quackenbush, Jannette. "Moonville Tunnel Brakeman." Ohio Ghost Stories, Legends, and Haunts (hauntedhocking.com). Accessed on March 9, 2025.

Staff Writer. "David Keeton." *The Hocking Sentinel*. July 8, 1886.

Staff Writer. "Many Legends of Ghosts Come from Ohio Hills." *The Circleville Herald*. October 17, 1978.

Staff Writer. "Old Citizen Killed—Criminal Notes." *The Cincinnati Enquirer*. June 29, 1886.

Staff Writer. "The ghost of Moonville." *Chillicothe Gazette*. January 23, 1895.

COLLINGWOOD SCHOOL FIRE *(Collingwood)*

Cakes, Christina. "My Haunted History, The Collinwood School Fire." HubPages (discover.hubpages.com). June 19, 2019

No author. "Horrors and Hauntings of the Collinwood School Fire." American Hauntings (americanhauntingsink.com). Accessed on January 30, 2025.

No author. "The Collinwood Fire, 1908." The Collingwood Fire, 1908 (collinwoodfire.org). Accessed on January 30, 2025.

No author. "Collinwood School Fire." Encyclopedia of Cleveland History (case.edu). Accessed on January 30, 2025.

FRANKENSTEIN'S CASTLE *(Kettering)*

No Author. "The story behind Frankenstein's Castle at Hills & Dales." Dayton Local (daytonlocal.com). October 13, 2015.

Powell, Lisa. "Dayton Legends: The long-told tales behind Kettering's 'Witch's Tower.'" *Dayton Daily News* (daytondailynews.com). October 4, 2022.

Quackenbush, Jannette. "Patterson's Tower." Ohio Ghost Stories, Legends, and Haunts (hauntedhocking.com). Accessed on March 16, 2025.

SPRING HOUSE GAZEBO *(Cincinnati)*

Brookbank, Sarah. "The ghost of Eden Park is 'definitely out there' 90 years after she was murdered." *The Cincinnati Enquirer.* October 27, 2017.

Nieforth, Joseph. "George Remus." Finda a Grave (findagrave.com). Accessed on March 29, 2025.

No Author. "Augusta Imogene Brown Remus." Find a Grave (findagrave.com). Accessed on March 29, 2025.

Staff Writer. "Insanity Only Defense Plea, Court Holds in Memorandum." *The Cincinnati Enquirer.* December 21, 1927.

Tran, Tram Anh. "The Ghost of Eden Park." *The News Record* (newsrecord.org). November 1, 2024.

About Jessica Freeburg

Jessica Freeburg is an internationally published author, history nerd, and researcher of the unexplained. She has written a wide variety of books, ranging from graphic novels to paranormal fiction and nonfiction, with a focus on creepy legends and dark moments from history.

As the founder of Ghost Stories Ink, Jessica has performed paranormal investigations at reportedly haunted locations across the US. She has appeared in documentaries and shows on such networks as the Travel Channel and Amazon Prime—talking about ghosts and haunted places—and can often be heard cohosting the wildly popular podcast *Darkness Radio*.

You can learn more about Jessica's work at her website, jessicafreeburg.com.

About Natalie Fowler

Natalie Fowler, once a practicing attorney, is now an award-winning author and ghost writer. Natalie's published works include nonfiction books on poignant—though sometimes dark—historical events and haunting legends. She is the researcher and historian for Ghost Stories Ink and has led paranormal investigations at some of the most notoriously haunted locations in the country. Inspired by the concept of spirit rescue, she cofounded a paranormal group called Paranormal Services Cooperative and has published accounts of her work as a medium in this field. You can learn more about her work and publications at nataliefowler.com.

The Story of AdventureKEEN

We are an independent nature and outdoor activity publisher. Our founding dates back more than 40 years, guided then and now by our love of being in the woods and on the water, by our passion for reading and books, and by the sense of wonder and discovery made possible by spending time recreating outdoors in beautiful places.

It is our mission to share that wonder and fun with our readers, especially with those who haven't yet experienced all the physical and mental health benefits that nature and outdoor activity can bring.

#bewellbeoutdoors